Your Man & His Mother

Annette Annechild

Your Man
&
His Mother

Annette Annechild

LONGMEADOW PRESS

Published by Longmeadow Press
201 High Ridge Road, Stamford, CT 06904

Cover design by Mike Stromberg

Library of Congress Cataloging-in-Publication Data

Annechild, Annette.
　Your man and his mother / Annette Annechild.—1st ed.
　　p.　　cm.
　ISBN 0-681-41466-9
　1. Mothers and sons.　2. Men—Psychology
3. Mothers—Psychology.　I. Title.
BF723.M55A56　　1992　　　　　　　　　　　　92–3246
155.9'24—dc20　　　　　　　　　　　　　　　　CIP

Printed in U.S.A.

First Edition

0　9　8　7　6　5　4　3　2　1

For Dr. J. S. Khalsa,
Whose life is a testament to the evolution of man—
With Love . . .

We must dream our dreams into reality—
With open hearts, we can change the world. . . .

Contents

Part III: The Controllers

Part IV: The Neglected

Part V: The Overwhelmed

Part VI: Conclusion

Foreword

"The truth is, it's his mom. He's angry at her for not protecting him from his father's beatings and he can never admit it, so he lashes out at me."

"Because his mother left him at an early age, he never connected again to any woman, not even me and it has been 12 years."

"His mother is in our relationship all the time, she lives there like a ghost. She raised five kids and worked and kept the house clean, made meals, everything. He always throws her up to me and I just cannot do it, I'll never be her."

"You know he was beaten by his mother when he was a kid. She hit him over the head with a board. Have you seen the scar? He is afraid to speak up to me or argue with me, I never know how he feels, he is so afraid of being hurt, sometimes I think he does not feel."

"He calls his mother daily. It is like he is married to her, ever since his father died. If I go over to his house on Friday or Saturday night because we are supposed to spend the evening together and his mother calls, he will stay on the phone for over an hour with me sitting there. Or, if it is Thanksgiving or Christmas, he goes to spend them with her, not with me."

I am struck by how often in sessions, my female clients want to talk about "his mother," before I even ask. There is no doubt that insight into a man's relationship with his mother, the first woman in his life, can lead to insight about his relationship to the women in his life at present. Annette and I have spent countless therapy hours working with this "woman" who is not present in the session, but very much present in her son's life and in the relationship we are treating. A young boy watching his mother, learns about women and how men are supposed to relate to them.

Annette Annechild delineates a variety of mothering styles in her book and then through case examples suggests how these styles can have an effect on a man, and his relationship towards women.

It is important to keep in mind that there are numerous and mixed styles of mothering. It is also important to note that one *cannot* say for certain that any particular mothering style creates a *specific* type of man. There are too many other influences at play.

In *Your Man & His Mother*, Annette Annechild lists fifteen different "types" of mothers and presents case scenarios of how each "type" of mothering affected a man and his relationship to a female partner. Each chapter begins with a brief overview of the early relationship of the couple and the early relationship the man had with his mother. In "The Clues," the reader is given ideas as to how the woman in each case example could have picked up early clues regarding her man's behavior. Finally, Annette discusses from her own life experience, and from treating these couples in relationship counseling, how an intervention can take place; and suggests how the couple can begin to work together to overcome the past influences and current responses that are detrimental to their relationship.

Annette's goal in this book is to open women's eyes and hearts to look beyond their partner and into his childhood. This book is a way to gain a deeper understanding of the actions and reactions they see in him today.

CAROLYN COSTIN M.S., MFCC
March, 1992

Acknowledgments

The idea for this book was a gift in the night. It was a concept I had felt for some time, then suddenly one morning it appeared as a title in my mind. From that moment on, it had a life of its own. . . . I called my favorite person in publishing, Adrienne Ingrum at Waldenbooks. She loved the concept, improved the title, and enthusiastically agreed to publish it. Her sensitivity to the material and sharp editorial judgment are reflected throughout this book. It was a pleasure and a privilege to work with her once again.

My manager and great friend, Andrea Capone, was the liaison of this East/West venture. She was there every step of the way, from developing the concept to directing the cover shoot to line editing the final manuscript. Her excellent editorial skills and excruciating attention to detail made this a better book. Her commitment to this project was unwavering. My appreciation of her quick mind and sensitive soul is enormous. In the most trying of times, her marvelous wit got us through. . . .

I would also like to thank my dear friend, Carolyn Costin, whose presence is also felt throughout this book. Her incredible insight and understanding of family dynamics have made her a leader in her field. Her brilliance as a therapist is matched only by her greatness as a person.

In addition, many thanks to Leonora Tint, my longtime friend and mentor, for her succinct and inspiring contributions. When I got stuck, one phone call to her and I was back on my way; thanks also to Marilyn Jaynes for her patient and perfect typing of this manuscript (my apologies once again for the unreadable handwriting!); to Mary Colacurcio and the Alumni Association and Library Staff of California State University at San Bernardino—their research assistance and kind support of this alumnia is greatly appreciated; to photographer David Guilburt, hair and makeup stylist Tamie Stanbury, and manicurist Nancy Schrillo for their excellent work on the cover photo; to my good friends and family, Bruce Martin, Fredda Kurtz, Leslie Goldstein, Bruce Rays, Dr. Terry Sereno, Dr. Roger Girion, Arlene Meyer, Swami

Satchidananda, Tina Farris, Carrie and Tony Gia-
chetti, Anne and Frank Viscardi, Jean Holdampf,
Barbara Tint, Gary Liss, Lisa Herrell, Jerry Laks,
Evelyn and Cois Byrd, Ed and Eileen Friedman, Janet
Marvin Falbo, Barbara and Joe Tranchito, and all my
friends in Malibu. Your love and support help me
through the project of daily living, and each of you in
your way helped me write this book.

Finally, a heartfelt thanks to all those who gener-
ously shared their stories so that others may learn
from their experiences; and especially to the memory
of Russell Bennett, whose life teaches me still; and to
S.J.—my eight-year-old inspiration.

Introduction

The premise for this book emerged from two areas close to my heart: my love life and my life's work. At thirty-six years old, I went back to school for a master's degree in psychology and, at the same time, reentered the dating scene; both were intensely educative experiences.

As I studied and learned about patterns of behavior and the psychodynamic theories of the *origins* of those behaviors, I knew I had found a field that would fascinate me forever. It made so much sense to me that what we experience as children largely determines how we view the world. If we never explore those early experiences, we may repeat, throughout our lives, behaviors that may not be working for us as adults.

As I began to date, I found a remarkable difference between men who had explored their pasts and those who had not. Sometimes I was confused by a man's behavior, but the more I applied what I was learning in school to what I was experiencing in life, the more I understood them. When a man had unresolved issues with his mother, he had unresolved issues with women in general, and how that manifested in our relationship became more and more predictable.

It is important for me to state clearly that I appreciate men wholly. Taking their mother relationship into consideration has enabled me to love them more, for it has helped me accept what they can give and forgive them for what they cannot. The goal here, then, is to understand *more* about the opposite sex, not less.

This book is an offering to positive change. It is dedicated to a deeper, more spiritual understanding of the special men in our lives. It has been said, "Men rule the world, and women rule the men." If that is at all true, let the power of both be guided by kindness and love. . . .

ANNETTE ANNECHILD
March 1992
Malibu, California

1

Why His Mother Matters

Every man begins his life in the same place. His mother carries him inside her womb, ushers him into the world, and in most cases feeds and nurtures him throughout his young life. To him, this person is not just a woman, it's *his mother*. It follows, then, that his mother would have a great influence on him, particularly on how he chooses and relates to women. Certainly, each man's individual personality and life experiences will determine what he does with his mother's input. Some men react against their mothers, choosing a mate who is a total opposite.

Others attempt to re-create that first relationship with the women they encounter throughout their lives. Whatever the case, you can be sure that her influence is *there*. If you love this man, knowing about his mother can only help you understand him better. Thinking about what life was like for him as a child can often shed light on his present behavior.

Childhood affects us all in a profound way. We were so completely vulnerable at those early stages, so open to input, that we stored millions of impressions both about ourselves and the opposite sex. These impressions become a belief system that may or may not be correct or good for us to hold on to. By examining our past and appreciating how our particular input affected us, we can, hopefully, free ourselves from old thoughts, feelings, and behaviors that no longer serve us.

Obviously, some people come from families where love and support were sufficiently available. But many of us come from families that struggled to provide us with adequate attention, reinforcement, love, and security. Today, these families are referred to as "dysfunctional." The children who come from these families often struggle with low self-esteem, guilt, fear of success, sexual dysfunction, fears of abandonment, and issues with intimacy.

Childhood forms us in a very real way, and it is our nature to seek what is familiar. For example, that is why children of alcoholics often seek alcoholic partners and children of abusers sometimes marry abusers themselves. What breaks the cycle is *understanding*, both of ourselves and the family from which we evolved. Our relationship with our opposite-sex parent lays the very foundation for how we will be with, and what we will expect from, a partner. The influence of that first relationship is so deep and so profound that our lifetime interactions with the opposite sex may, to some extent, be simply reflections or distortions of that which we have known before.

This pattern of continually re-creating our past was illuminated for me time and time again as I resumed dating. Often I would be completely confused by a man's behavior. Those I considered close would somehow disappear, seemingly for no reason, while others I could not discourage no matter what I did. I felt even though I was in the relationship, I was somehow not the *only* female player. Gradually I began to identify that other female presence as his mother. As I put my theory to work, I was amazed at the accuracy with which I could predict the problems and patterns in a relationship based on the man's relationship with his mother. Then I began my internship for my California Marriage, Family and Child Counselor license. During the next two years I worked with a large number of women between the ages of seventeen and fifty. Time and time again, as we examined their boyfriend's or husband's mother-/son relationships, we could understand better what he was now doing and why.

This is not meant, in any way, to imply that people are necessarily frozen in patterns determined by their past; but very often, unless the person has worked through this primary relationship, they continue to be strongly influenced by it. Certainly there are men who were raised with just the right mixture of love and independence, but in my experience, both as a woman and as a professional, these men are more the exception than the rule.

As I interviewed past and present clients as well as friends and colleagues, I was struck by the eagerness of both men and women to share their stories—to understand and to be understood.

As their stories unfolded, it became clear to me that there was a universal quality to their personal experiences. When writing their stories, rather than use pseudonyms, I felt the use of "he" and "she" better expressed that universal quality. Eventually specific styles of mothering were clarified and the subsequent patterns of behaviors identified, many of the women recognized their men and felt relieved that "they weren't crazy"—the vague feelings they could never fully explain became more concrete and understandable in light of their man's dynamics. As they became more confident of their feelings, many were able to begin to act, rather than to react, within the relationship. By not taking their partner's actions so personally, they were able to keep their hearts more open and to respond to their man on a deeper level.

For example, a man who is a "distancer," perhaps as a result of an overly enmeshed, suffocating mother, may often leave his partner feeling insecure, "not good enough," and abandoned. In response, she may chase harder, which simply heightens the dance of distancer/pursuer. When she finally explodes and lashes out, she confirms to the distancer that he is right—it is *not safe* to stop running, and the pattern stays in place, more firmly entrenched than ever. A woman who instead recognizes that pattern and internalizes the reality that it is *not* really about *her* can instead back off and *engage* the distancer. When the pursuer stops pursuing, the dance is forced to change. When it does, the old pattern collapses, thereby creating space for fresh new energy and growth.

My hope in writing this book is that it will help you revitalize your relationship by providing new insights and understanding. Even if your man is not interested in changing and doesn't believe he was affected by his mother, it can still work for you. *Your* awareness can influence *your* behavior, and that in itself will create change. We can never successfully change the other person. True change comes from within. We can only work on ourselves. This book is a tool with which to begin that work.

The best way to begin is to read each chapter of this book, not only the one that seems to relate to your man. Very often his mother will be a *combination* of types. She may have been distant *and* critical or depressed *and* overprotective. She may have been somewhat anxious but more often childlike. By reading each chapter you will be able to recognize the different patterns that fit your man and be able to apply the interventions. Remember, awareness is best used as a *tool*, not a weapon. If you keep your heart open, this information could change your life.

2

Mothers and Sons: The Research and the Findings

To make this book as thorough as possible, I have included this chapter, which explores the research to date on the subject of mother and sons. Unlike the rest of the book, which is based on case studies, this chapter examines the scientific research conducted by the psychological community.

The most striking element when you explore the research conducted on the relationship between men and their mothers is how little there is of it. In the past twenty years only a small number of studies have been published in psychology literature. Clearly this is a fertile area for further study. Another striking feature of the research is the overwhelming support for the theory that the mother/son relationship is truly the tie that binds. What follows is a brief overview of the studies that have been done and their findings.

An Overview

Taken as a whole, these studies explore many aspects of the nature of mother/son relationships. In one study, patterns of mother/son interactions are compared with the sons' behavior level of aggression and withdrawal. In another, a man's attitude toward women in the labor force is found to be correlated to his mother's work status. In other research, the intimacy of a single-parent household is examined, as well as the relationship between a mother's moral judgment and those of her son. A man's mate choice is found to be connected with his mother's nativity in one study, and in yet another, submissive behavior by a mother is linked to dominant behavior by her son. A mother's educational expectations of her son are found to influence his academic performance, and how at peace a woman is with her ex-husband is found to affect her relationship with her son directly. The pervasive and long-term damage caused by a mother's sexual abuse of her son is illustrated in the research, and how a mother communicates differently with her daughters and sons is also explored.

Finally, the effect of a mother's mood is found to have a dramatic effect on her relationship with her son. What follows is a further description of each of these studies, including who conducted them, when they were conducted, and where they were published.

In 1978 a study was conducted by Judy Genshaft at Ohio State University. Her research, titled "The Empirical Study of Mother and Son Interactions," which was published in *Social Behavior and Personality,* points toward a correlation between styles of mothering and behavior traits in sons. Ms. Genshaft compared patterns of mother/son interactions with their son's observed levels of aggression and withdrawal. She concluded that some differences in mother/son interactions seem related to aggression/withdrawal in children.

In 1982, Brian Powell and LaLa Carr Steelman conducted a study that was published in the *Journal of Marriage and Family.* Their research is titled "Testing an Under Tested Comparison: Maternal Effects on Sons' and Daughters' Attitudes Toward Women in the Labor Force." They explored the relationship between a mother's work status and educational level to the sex-role attitudes (toward women in the labor force) of her offspring. They found that the association between maternal characteristics and their children's attitudes toward women in the labor force is stronger for sons than for daughters. They explain this difference in this way: "Development of attitudes toward the opposite sex may arise from interaction with the opposite sex parent who serves as a role model. By contrast, attitudes towards one's own sex are possibly shaped by exposure to many alternative role models. Under these conditions, males would be affected by their mother's status characteristics and females would be affected by their father's status characteristics." In addition, they state, "Males may carry their stamp pads of expected female behavior learned in early contact with the mother, with them into adulthood." This directly supports the concept on which this book is based: Mothers greatly affect their sons and that effect is certainly passed down to the next woman in his life—you.

In 1984 Thomas Kenmore and Loretta Wineberg conducted an interesting study that was published in the *Clinical Social Work Journal*. This research, titled "The Tie That Binds: A Clinical Perspective on Divorced Mother and Adolescent Sons," examines the intense intimacy that sometimes develops between mothers and sons after a divorce. They describe this intimacy as an attempt to adapt to the loss of the husband/father and as a defense against mourning. (In Chapter 8, "The Romantic Mother," a case study is presented that illustrates this occurrence.) The Kenmore/Wineberg article describes the problem this intimacy can cause in adolescent sons. It also describes treatment strategies to loosen the bond and to reengage both the mother and son in the process of mourning.

The next study, conducted by Manuel Leon in 1984 at California State University at Sacramento, illustrates the direct influence of a mother's thinking on her son's thinking process. This research, titled "Rules

Mothers and Sons Use to Integrate Intent and Damage Information in Their Moral Judgments," compared the rules mothers and sons used to assign punishment as a function of intent and damage. He concluded that the similarity between rules used by mother and their sons was remarkable.

A particularly interesting study in 1984 was conducted by Davor Jedlicka at the University of Texas. His study, called "Indirect Parental Influence on Mate Choice: A Test of the Psychoanalytic Theory," which was published in *Journal of Marriage in the Family*, explained the influence of parents on their children's choice of a marriage partner. Nativity of fathers and mothers was compared with the nativity of their children's spouses on each of the 32,000 marriage licenses issued in Hawaii between 1978 and 1980. He concluded, "Despite a few exceptions, two general tendencies are indicated by the data. First, at least with respect to nativity, mate choice is considerably more influenced by mothers than by fathers. Second, mate choice of sons is more influenced by mothers that is mate choice of daughters. And mate choice of daughters is more influenced by fathers than mate choice of sons. In general, these data support the psychoanalytic theory of indirect parental influence on mate choice." He concludes by saying "Given the encouraging results of this study, it can be concluded that the opposite-sex parent serves as a guiding image in mate selection. Therefore, the resemblance between the opposite-sex parent and the spouse occurs more frequently than expected by chance." Again, this is support for our premise of how connected you are to the mother of the man you love.

In the *Journal of Consulting and Clinical Psychology* in

1985, a study was published by Randy Phelps and Mark Slater titled "Sequential Interactions that Discriminate High and Low Problem Single Mother/Son Dyads.* This study looked at single mothers and their sons and found that in the dyads categorized as "high problem," submissive communications from mothers elicited dominant responses from their sons; also, dominant communications from sons elicited submissive responses from their mothers. In dyads considered "low problem," this was not the case.

In 1986, Rachel Seginer published an article, "Mother's Behavior and Son's Performance: An Initial Test of Academic Achievement Path Model," in the *Merrill-Palmer Quarterly*. She conducted a path analysis of the data collected on 107 fifth-grade boys. Her results indicated that "A mother's educational expectations were strongly related to their son's academic performance." Again, in this research the link between a mother and her son is highlighted.

In 1988, in the *Journal of Divorce*, Robert Greene and Leslie Leigh published their research titled "Mothers' Behavior and Sons' Adjustment Following Divorce." They studied two aspects of the mother-son relationships (maternal support and coercion) as reported by the son. The extent to which the mother's attitude toward her ex-spouse might be affecting her interactions with her son was also assessed. Their results suggest "that eighteen to thirty-nine months after parental separation, a mother's attitude toward her former mate is related to how supportive or coercive

*Dyad refers to a group of two.

her son reports her to be in their relationship. Like-
wise, how coercive the mother is perceived to be is
related to teacher ratings of the son's levels of aggression in school."

In a somewhat different but related study, Ronald
Krug in 1989 published a study in *Child Abuse and
Neglect* called "Adult Male Report of Childhood Sexual Abuse by Mothers: Case Descriptions, Motiva-
tions, and Long-Term Consequences." He presents
case histories of eight men sexually abused as children by their mothers. "As adults, each of these men
experienced difficulty maintaining an intimate emotional and sexual relationship with one person and
most presented with some degree of depression. Sub-
stance abuse was present in five of the eight cases."
This was yet another testament to the pervasive damage caused by abuse and the power of that primary
relationship to heal or to wound.

In 1989, Robyn Fivush conducted a study at Emory
University that was published in *Sex Roles* and called
"Exploring Sex Differences in the Emotional Content
of Mother/Child Conversations About the Past." She
explored ways in which eighteen mothers and their
2½-year-old children discussed emotional aspects of
past experiences. Half of the children were boys, half
were girls. "With daughters, mother focused more on
the positive emotions and tended not to attribute
negative emotions to the child; with sons, positive
and negative emotions were discussed equally. Mothers never discussed anger with daughters, but did
with sons. Mother-daughter conversations often discussed the causes and consequences of emotions.

The author does not speculate as to what effect that has on these children as adults, but it may allude to the special relationship that is evident between mothers and sons. Perhaps mothers are inclined to discuss subjects more openly and extensively with their sons, subjects they protect their daughters from, such as anger.

Finally, in 1989, Ernest Jouriles, Christopher Murphy, and Daniel Leary published their study "Effects of Maternal Mood on Mother-Son Interaction Patterns" in the *Journal of Abnormal Child Psychology*. They evaluated the impact of maternal mood on mother-son interaction patterns. Their study involved forty boys and their mothers. Mood inductions performed on the mothers were followed by mother-son interactions that were observed. "During the negative mood condition mothers issued fewer positive statements toward their children and engaged in less verbal interaction. In addition, children were less compliant with maternal commands during the negative mood condition." They conclude, "In sum, the present results suggest that maternal mood influences maternal interactions with pre-school children. These findings illustrate the importance of understanding the role of situational factors in parent-child interaction and suggest that clinical efforts to enhance the quality of parent-child interaction may need to address situational determinants of parenting, particularly factors that adversely affect parental mood." Anyone who has had children will certainly agree with the logic in that. An unhappy parent is less likely to respond positively to his or her child. Children, of course, often pick up on a parent's mood and act or react accordingly.

All of this research supports what every therapist I know already believes, that we are all greatly influenced by our childhood. This book is not a psychology textbook. It is, instead, an attempt to capture what I have heard, seen, and felt. I have tried to listen with my heart and to follow my instincts. Opposite-sex parents affect us in a very potent way. He may be your boyfriend or husband now, but he was her son *first*. Who she was and how she treated him is his legacy. What he does with that legacy is up to him, and what you do with the relationship is ultimately up to *you*. He does not necessarily have to work on his relationship with his mother in order to work it out with you. All of the information you gather can provide insight, and that can enable you both to communicate more effectively. The more you know, the more you can understand. Hopefully, the more you can understand, the more you can love . . .

3

Styles of Mothering

Mothers reading this book may wonder if there is any way to do it really "right." Certainly, raising children is no easy task, and no one should expect themselves to do it flawlessly. We each do it the best way we can. The happier and more balanced you are, the better your relationship with your children will be. The purpose of this book is not to criticize mothers but instead to help women better understand sons. Most of us have a bit of each of these mothers in us. Who hasn't been overprotective at times, or anxious or even deceptive perhaps? The more pronounced these traits are, the more influence they exert. For instance, the mother who is *always* anxious will raise a different son than one who is occasionally upset.

What a son manifests with his mother's influence also depends on his own personality, initiative, and life circumstance. Following is a brief description of sixteen different styles of mothering. These are based on patterns I have come to recognize again and again. Obviously many more styles exist and many combinations of different styles. As you read through the styles and the following chapters, you might recognize your man in more than one case study. By combining the information that applies, you will be able to piece together a picture of *why* he is like he is and hopefully then begin to understand him better and communicate with him more effectively.

Sons of Distant Mothers

This relationship is characterized by a lack of warmth. The mother may have done all the *tasks* of mothering, but in truth she never really connected with her son emotionally. Perhaps something in her own life caused her to cut off from her deepest feelings, so it was impossible for her to open her heart to her son. Motherhood itself may have overwhelmed her, or perhaps her family of origin struggled with the same problem. Whatever the cause, the outcome was an inability to connect. This mother/son relationship often has very little physical contact and is permeated with a cold, vacant feeling. Often the child will feel responsible for the mother's distance. Initially he probably ran after his mother's love, then he may have convinced himself he didn't need it and eventually closed down—just like his mother. As an adult, he may believe he is unlovable and find it hard to trust that love can ever come to him.

Sons of Deceptive Mothers

The prominent feature of the deceptive relationship is the existence of some sort of secret that is part of the mother's life. This mother is burdened with a secret that may involve alcohol, drugs, an affair, or some element of a hidden past. This secret creates a chaotic, insecure environment that is usually permeated with guilt. Unable to be intimate even with herself, this mother cannot possibly extend intimacy to her son. He often grows up feeling responsible for and frustrated by a situation he cannot understand or control. His trust factor is usually low as his world is perceived as unsafe and uncertain. In future relationships he will often feel on the outside rather than as a true part of something. As his mother's first allegiance was to her secret, so his first allegiance will usually be to himself. He cannot trust that things are always as they appear. This mother/son relationship is generally characterized by bursts of affection and periods of distance. He may not have known the exact nature of his mother's secret, but he was immersed in the uneasiness it created.

The Smothering Mother

This is a mother/son relationship that knows no boundaries. Her love envelops him, and there is no escape. This mother barges into the most intimate corners of her son's life. He is never allowed to develop independently or leave her. If he goes against her, she punishes him with guilt. He senses that he can never escape from this overwhelming presence. Her love is a hungry tiger that is always chasing him.

The Depressed Mother

The depressed mother is not only sad, but also hopeless. Very often this is accompanied by disturbed eating and sleeping patterns. One description of depression is "anger turned inward"; whatever the cause, its presence can be a living hell. Each day is a struggle, and the family of a depressed person struggles as well. A child's reaction to a parent's depression can be a taking on of depressive symptoms or just the reverse, a denial of all depressive feelings. In either case, the child is profoundly affected. Fortunately, there is help for those suffering from depression. Therapy, sometimes coupled with medication, can free a person to experience and enjoy life once again.

The Romantic Mother

When the father is absent or distant, a relationship can develop between a mother and son that has the aura of romance. They become each other's favorite friend, they prefer each other's company. When the father is present, they might often team up against him and/or share a private communication from which he is excluded. On some level she may consider her son to be "her man," and she might view other women as competition. This mother may creates a son who has only fantasy female adult relationships that don't hold up in the real world.

The "Perfect" Mother

In Chapter 9 we meet the mother who tries too hard. She does everything with complete attention and expects perfection from herself and those around her. The family is her corporation, and she is a vigilant CEO. She is dedicated to detail and is proud to be successful in many visible areas of her life. To her son, she is an icon. He believes nobody could ever take her place.

The Critical Mother

A legacy of criticism can be passed down from generation to generation, from family to family. Life is so imperfect that if you are in a critical mode, there is *always* something to criticize. Critical people are unhappy people, and their worst victim will more than likely be themselves. This is not always easy to recognize, because it is often an evasive, subtle, negative self-judgment that is not verbalized.

Here is a person to whom all things appear equal, no matter how trivial they truly are. They can be as upset over being ten minutes late as they can over losing a job. It's as though they are filled with unhappiness and any minor incident can open the spout. A parent with a critical attitude toward a child often expects the child to accomplish or become what they themselves never could. The child may become successful, but is often resentful of the constant pressure applied by the parent. This unhappiness is often passed down again in the form of criticism to the next generation.

The Compulsive Mother

When discussing compulsive behavior, it is important to clarify the different levels of this condition. Many of us feel we have compulsive and/or obsessive traits. We may feel highly motivated about our work and refer to ourselves as "compulsive" about doing it well, or we may have something on our mind we continually think about for a while and tell a friend, "I'm obsessing over this situation." Clearly, this would not be considered a true disorder if the tendency is mild and does not interfere with daily living in a negative way.

A person who does have obsessive-compulsive disorder is in distress. There is a difference between obsessions and compulsions. Obsessions are intrusive thoughts that occur again and again. The person tries to stop or ignore the thoughts but cannot. Compulsions are intentional behaviors or rituals that are repeated over and over. The person intentionally performs the behaviors as a way of reducing tension. Both obsessions and compulsions interfere in a negative way with the person's life.

A less severe condition is "obsessive-compulsive personality disorder." People with this personality disorder are driven to strive for perfection. They are generally rigid and inflexible; details and a quest for order control their lives, and they may insist that others behave this way as well. Decisions are difficult for this personality type, as they are afraid of doing the wrong thing. Often they are so consumed with either their work or some sort of organizational task that they have no time for pleasure or friends. A true "workaholic" would fall into this category.

A mother who is troubled with any of these conditions will certainly affect her children. The child may inherit the tendency and become compulsive as well. The opposite could also be true: There may be a rejection of the characteristics, and the child may go toward a highly unstructured life. In any case, knowing about his mother can help you understand why he is like he is.

The Childlike Mother

This mother is the eternal baby of the family. Instead of this woman protecting her son, he, along with everyone else, protects her. She is usually sweet and innocent but incapable of truly taking on the role of mother. Instead she enjoys a life of blind denial. She can be manipulated easily and is more like a sibling than a parent. The father is usually the strong leader of the family. As an adult, the son may view women as sweet, incapable figures and himself as the powerful protector of his home.

The Abusive Mother

I feel it is important to preface this particular chapter with a discussion of how a mother comes to create such a negative relationship with her son. Certainly no one sets out with the intention of becoming an abusive parent. Most abusers have been abused themselves, and abuse often appeared acceptable in their earliest environment. If a person is raised with screaming and hitting as reactions to everyday problems, that is what they will understand to be normal methods of coping. Remember, we all tend to repeat patterns, and we gravitate toward the familiar. The legacy of abuse is present in thousands of families in our country today. Understanding the effect of this legacy on your man can help you overcome it together. Encouraging him to seek professional help is a wise move. Abuse, whether it is physical, emotional, or psychological, is extremely damaging. The scars are deep and long-lasting. Many of my clients have forgiven their abusive parent but still struggle with the residual damage. Understandably, trust is a big issue for those who have been abused; do not expect it quickly or take it lightly. Also, there are very often feelings of self-doubt—wondering if they "made it up" or are "imagining" that it happened. This can be heightened by the rest of the family being in denial about it. Often this is accompanied by self blame, feeling as though if it did happen, it was *their* fault, and they somehow deserved it. These issues are best dealt with in a therapeutic environment. Do try to be supportive; do not try to take on the job yourself.

The Absent Mother

Without the reality of this crucial relationship between mother and son, either through death or desertion, the image of a mother is often manufactured. Discovering what *his* created image is can help you learn a lot about where he is coming from. Many children with an absent parent believe they *caused* their parent's disappearance, and they may experience deep guilt and regret throughout their lives.

The Mother Who Abandons

Unlike the absent mother, whom he has never known, this is a mother who was there, then gone. Here is a son who experienced his mother's love and then had it ripped away. This abandonment can be due to divorce or desertion but also can be due to illness or death. Very often a young child in this situation believes it is his fault, as if the mother left *because of* him. As an adult, this man may have difficulty believing he will not be left again. Unfortunately, often his own actions can make this a self-fulfilling prophecy. The loss of a mother at an early age can create a deep fearfulness in a person coupled with the suspicion that things will never be good for long. Often, the better things get, the more uncomfortable he will become.

The Overprotective Mother

This relationship is characterized by an overwhelming sense of impending doom. Here is a mother who doesn't hold her son's hand, she *clutches* it. Her core belief is that the world is not a safe place and that she must protect her son from it. She anticipates his needs and responds before he is hardly conscious of them. Nothing is ever easy or flowing; fear and doubt guide the relationship. This mother worries about her son constantly, and her negative attention often prevents him from taking chances and reaching his full potential. This mother is filled with love for her child, her motives are pure, but somewhere along the way, life overwhelmed her. Now she tries to protect her son from that same fate. Very often the son also begins to believe that the world is not safe and is thankful his mother is there to protect him. Another part of him may resent his mother and the way her fear has kept him a prisoner in his own life. Unfortunately, some of these sons take no chances and create a small, limited world for themselves.

The Peacemaker

The peacemaker has only one goal in life: to keep the peace. She wants a smooth life without the discomfort of freely expressed emotions. On one hand, this can appear to create a pleasant, calm environment within the home; on the other hand, it can leave the family, particularly the children, unprepared to deal with life's inevitable ups and downs. There is an unacknowledged uneasiness in the peacemaker's family because the negative emotions have not been allowed to surface. Instead, they remain alive and unprocessed in the psyche of the family.

The Anxious Mother

The anxious mother is similar to the over-protective mother as the core belief of both is that the world is not a safe place. The difference lies in that the over-protective mother believes she can save her son from harm, while the anxious mother believes no one can save either of them. Free-floating anxiety fills the house and bad news is always expected. When it comes, it is always exaggerated and she is always overwhelmed. He has no sense that she can truly take care of him and life is always tinged with fear.

Part I

The Distancers

4

Distant Mothers' Sons

"I always wanted more from him—and I couldn't understand why he wouldn't give it. We'd been together for almost a year and he still hadn't said that he loved me."

The Love Story

She met him in the gym. She was in there one night after work, tired but determined to get through her routine. She went to use the leg press at exactly the same time he did. He was gracious and insisted she go first. He stood and watched her as he waited. She could feel his eyes on her. As they alternated sets, they started talking, and before long he asked her to go for coffee afterward. As it turned out, he usually worked out in the morning, which was why they had never seen each other before. He was single, twenty-eight years old, and just out of law school. She told him she had just turned thirty. When he asked her out for Saturday night, she was thrilled. They went to dinner and a movie and had a great time. She was a little surprised he never held her hand during the movie. She had wanted to grab his arm during a scary part of the movie, but stopped herself, though she didn't know why. He didn't touch her at all. He didn't kiss her good night, but she told herself that she wasn't in any hurry either.

After that, they started to go out every weekend. They enjoyed each other's company, and they liked doing all the same things. Before long, she knew she was falling in love with him.

Months went by and still they had not been physically intimate. She knew he really liked her, but he was never really warm and affectionate with her. Finally she seduced him and got him into bed. It felt odd to be the aggressor, but she wanted so badly to bond with him on the deepest levels. He was wonderful in bed, but once it was over he was removed and distant. There was no pillow talk, no shared afterglow. He was back to business as usual. After that they became lovers on a regular basis, but it was always the same. It left her feeling empty and alone. She tried to talk to him about it, but he got frustrated with her and accused her of always wanting more from him. "Nothing is ever enough." She was frustrated, too: She did want more of him and couldn't understand why he couldn't give it to her. They had been together for almost a year, and he still hadn't told her he loved her. He seemed so far away at times. She loved him so much, it hurt her when he acted so distant. They started having a lot of fights. He said she was a nag and he was tired of her demands. She said she felt lonely and didn't believe he really cared for her. She wanted him to marry her—to take her in his arms and tell her he couldn't live without her. It just wasn't his style. Finally she gave him an ultimatum: She wanted a commitment or it was over. He couldn't take the pressure anymore, he told her. Maybe she was right—he wasn't really in love with her. He just didn't know anymore.

His Story

He could not remember much of his childhood. His mother cooked and cleaned, took him to school, and picked him up—she performed all the perfunctory duties. But he couldn't remember any displays of affection. No hugging or kissing him. He didn't ever remember her saying "I love you." He never saw his mother or father kiss, either. Everyone was always nice to each other in his house. There were no fights that he could remember. No screaming or yelling, like at some of his friends' houses. But not much laughing or talking, either. Their home was void of any emotional outbursts. When he would think back, he pictured his mother with a faraway look in her eyes, like she was always thinking about something else. She did tell him he was a good boy, and he knew he was. He got high grades in school, and he never went around with the rough crowd.

He dated one girl through most of high school, but he never slept with her. In fact, his first sexual experience was with an older girl he barely knew. When he got to college, he worked really hard. He knew he wanted to be a lawyer, and he wanted to be able to choose his law school. He didn't go home much at all. His parents called about once every two weeks to see how he was doing and if he had enough money. His mother would get on the line and they would exchange the same few sentences every time. He didn't miss his parents. He didn't miss anybody, really. He hung out with a few guys in his dorm and dated only occasionally. He got accepted to every law school he applied to and chose one out of state. Again, he studied hard and did well. He dated one girl for a while, but it ended when she started pressuring him to get married. He wanted school behind him before he thought about marriage. When he graduated he went to work for a law firm in the same city. He occasionally talked to his parents. He and his mother still exchanged the same four or five sentences. He liked his life, he supposed. He was glad to finally be a lawyer.

The Intervention

From the beginning, she was *reflecting* his behavior, rather than just being herself. On their first date, when she wanted to grab his arm, she didn't. When they said good night, she wanted to hug him, which she would normally do with all her friends, but his formal good night made her step back. While unimportant on the surface, this *is* important because she was already stifling herself, and would inevitably come to resent it. Had she enough confidence just to be herself, he might have begun modeling her familiarity and warmth. "I hope it's okay that I'm so touchy— it's just the way I am," she might have said. If he viewed her as just naturally warm and open with all her friends, including him, he might really enjoy it. Instead of pressuring *him* to be something he can't be, she might have just allowed herself to be herself and let him react however he did.

Her insecurity prevails, and it begins to dominate their time together. She pulls back, and there is now a tension in her when she is with him. She gets angry and behaves coldly toward him. In effect, this warm, loving woman has become his mother. He reacts by becoming even more his mother's son. At first he tries to appease her, then he decides he can never please her, so he shuts her out. When you truly love someone, the best thing you can do is keep your heart open and treat that person lovingly no matter what. If he or she doesn't respond in a way you like, you can either leave the person or love him or her anyway. To try to force the person to love you *your* way by withholding affection is a dead end. So many couples end up in a power struggle over love. They begin criticizing each other and, in reality, tearing down the very person they had wanted to love.

In this love story, she needs to stay in her own

shoes—she needs to be herself. That doesn't mean she can't lovingly communicate her needs. She can, but she must do it gently and with a lot of reinforcement. He needs to believe he *can* love her the way she wants to be loved. She must be on his side and help him get in touch with the feelings he lost long ago. It's better to go slowly with a man like this and perhaps date others if you are very unhappy with his degree of affection. Often, having a strong circle of friends and family can help you fill some of your needs, so that what he offers will be enough.

This couple came to therapy together and started to recognize how the differences in their mothering affected their expectations. She explained her own insecurities and need for attention, and he worked on his tendency to be distant and to withdraw. When each took responsibility for his or her part of the problem, the solutions became workable. She got back in touch with old friends she had not been involved with since he had become the center of her life. Soon she felt less needy and more like her old self. He loved the change in her and was able to hear her when she asked for *specific* things from him that he was capable of providing. As he talked more and more about his distant relationship with his mother, she understood it was not all about *her*. She began to believe he really did love her and that she didn't need to pressure him to say it all the time. Both of them grew personally as well as together, and the relationship eventually culminated in marriage. Once he felt truly secure with her and capable of making her happy, the wall came down, and his true desire for love emerged. She also grew as a person, believing more in her natural instincts and self-worth. He will probably never be as easily affectionate and touchy as she, but he can let himself enjoy her now, and she is secure that no matter what his *style* of loving, he truly loves her with all his heart.

The Clues

On their first date, she feels drawn to him and is surprised he doesn't make any attempt for physical contact. There's her first clue. His style right from the start is a bit removed. His pattern continues over the first months of dating. She is always hungry for a little more of him. Eventually she seduces him. There's nothing wrong with that in and of itself, but it is a clue to who he is. Here is a man who moves slowly with people, a man who is not easy with intimacy.

The relationship continues. Rather than recognize the clues to who *he* is, she starts feeling it must be something about her. She begins to feel insecure and then depressed and angry. As his emotional distance begins to affect her behavior, he pulls farther and farther away. She has plugged in to his old programming. She now acts coldly, and he begins believing he can never have a successful love relationship, that he can never make a woman happy. She finds out more about his past relationships, and the clues continue. He never talks about having a deep, intimate relationship with *anybody*. He dates a girl for a while, then she seems to disappear. He never expresses any strong emotions, either about the girl or about the loss of her. To her it seems his attention has always been focused on school and now his career. All of these clues are telling her he has never been able to connect. If she had asked about his mother, he probably would have described her in a superficial, unemotional way.

The biggest challenge in a relationship like this is not to take it all *personally*. If you love a man like this, you need to be patient. It's not that he doesn't love you, it's that he doesn't know how to *express* it. Having missed that deep primary exchange with his mother, it is foreign to him. Most likely, a wall went up when he couldn't get close to his mother, and that's the wall you need to climb over if you want him truly to let you in.

Do's

- Do be yourself right from the beginning and hold on to your self worth.
- Do ask questions and listen for past relationship patterns.
- Do lovingly communicate your needs.
- Do keep your own strong circle of friends and family.

Don'ts

- Don't play his game of withdrawal.
- Don't take his actions personally.
- Don't try to force him to love you *your* way.

5

Deceptive Mothers' Sons

"It was such a great beginning, then things began to fall apart. The harder I tried to be close to him, the more distant he became."

The Love Story

Months before she actually met him, she saw his picture. She was in the home of her workout partner and noticed a framed photo of her friend with his buddies on a biking trip. One of the men struck her immediately. He wasn't really handsome, but his energy seemed to pop out of the picture. She liked his looks and his spirit—she was on her way.

"Who is *he*?" she blurted out to her friend.

He was happy to oblige. "Why didn't I ever think

of him for you? He's terrific. He's thirty-four years old, never been married, a builder, very spiritual, a musician, works out hard, lots of fun. He lives up North in the mountains."

It all sounded great to her. They called right then and there. He was home, they chatted for over an hour; the connection felt magical. She would always remember that he had said, "It is so rare to talk to such a deep woman—it's hard to find people who are true."

Letters were next, then more calls. Each contact was better than the last. They understood each other, they laughed together. They agreed on a lot and enjoyed discussing it when they didn't.

They talked about their families—hers big and Italian, her parents still married after forty-five years. His mother had been an alcoholic for as long as he could remember. His parents had divorced when he was twelve, and his mother died when he was twenty. They talked about past relationships. She was thirty-two and had been married twice. He'd had two previous relationships—both for two years. They had ended, he said, because they weren't the right woman. She felt in her heart that she was.

There were gaps in the contact. Sometimes he didn't call when he said he would. Then suddenly he called and said he was arriving in two days and would be staying with their mutual friend. She rearranged her whole schedule, picked him up at the airport, made him a great dinner, and broke her own rule about not sleeping with a man right away. They had an incredibly romantic, fun weekend. Monday she had to go to work. He was waiting with roses when she returned. They talked about their goals and dreams. He said children gave purpose to life. She couldn't believe how perfect it all was—but she did. She went to work Tuesday; he borrowed her car to visit his uncle in a nearby town. He was late picking her up and seemed distracted. She let it slide. He said he was meeting his uncle for dinner that night and didn't invite her along. She understood.

He was leaving the next day. She had taken off early to be able to have a good-bye lunch with him. He came back from his dinner late, woke her up, and said he was really sorry but he had had such a great time reconnecting with his family that he was going to lunch with his uncle the next day. He never invited her—there would be no good-bye lunch. But he kissed her and hugged her—she tried to understand. She knew she could be overly sensitive and didn't want to overreact. They said a hurried good-bye in the morning. He left her beautiful notes. He called her when he got home.

He invited her up for a visit. She planned her vacation—a week up at his mountain house. As the vacation got closer, he seemed to retreat. She received fewer calls in which he sounded less excited about her coming. Finally, he said maybe a week was too long. He hadn't spent a full week with a woman in a long time. Maybe a few days would be better, and they could see how it went. Maybe she could drive all the way up instead of his meeting her as planned. She was heartbroken. She booked a trip to Mexico with a girlfriend instead. She drank tequila, watched pink sunsets, and longed for him. She almost just headed for his house, but called instead the minute she got home. It was Sunday night, at midnight, and a girl answered the phone. It wasn't his sister.

His Story

Raised by an alcoholic mother who couldn't be there for him, here is a man who learned to do it all alone. The alcoholic person by definition lives a life of deception. Alcohol warps a person's perception of reality, and alcoholics deceive everyone around them every day with their drinking. An alcoholic mother teaches self-centeredness every day by her example. She projects an inability to attain intimacy by being unable to offer the experience to her children. The child of an alcoholic grows up in a chaotic, insecure environment over which he has no control. He often feels responsible for the parent, rather than the other way around, and it is an impossible responsibility.

Some children of alcoholics become "fixers"; others become "distancers." Both learn to deny their real feelings because the pain of being abandoned by the parent is too great to bear. Their survival mechanism kicks in, and the pain becomes tolerable because it is buried. On the surface, this man functioned exceptionally well. He was generally sensitive and loving as long as he was not committed, as long as his life did not depend on another. To commit, to really surrender to love would duplicate the dependence he felt as a child. The potential for pain and loss would once again be present, and that is too much to bear for a psyche that is still overloaded with unprocessed grief.

Groups like Al-Anon and Adult Children of Alcoholics can make an enormous difference in the lives of these types of men. These groups are support systems where both men and women share their struggles and triumphs with these issues. But *he* has to want it. Your wanting it for him is never enough.

The Intervention

What can you possibly do with this type of man? You first have to recognize who they are and forget what you know they could be or what you want them to be. Falling in love with *potential* is a big mistake. In a man, what you see is what you get. Sure he can improve, but he is going to do it *his* way, when *he's* ready. All *you* can control is yourself. All along the way you have to check in with yourself and *trust* your feelings. When he didn't call when he said he would, she was hurt, but blamed herself for being overly sensitive. It is *not* being overly sensitive to expect people to do what they say or explain what happened. Had she confronted him about it right away, she might have found out more about him and about herself much sooner. Then she would have had the chance to decide if she wanted that type of man.

Moreover, had she taken into account his mother

issues she would have known to go slower. Here is a man who needs to make *friends* with a woman. He will be much more comfortable if he doesn't feel in over his head. This is someone with whom you need to be up front and clear with, but not demanding: "I am looking for a serious committed relationship—*but not necessarily with you.*" You must allow him to give what he can, when he can. He needs to pursue; you need to keep all other options open and let him know that you have. He may not like it on the surface, but it will keep him coming forward, instead of in his usual patterns of retreat.

The bad news is that often you may be disappointed with how much he is willing to give: When you retreat, he may let you go. The good news is that if and when these men do commit they generally are *very* committed. If they can break through their old patterns, their loving nature can emerge, and their deepest need for an intimate partner can surface. You can be a part of that if you choose to and if you master what may be *your* old patterns of chasing. In a marriage these men will probably require quite a bit of space, which means you need to stay involved with your own needs and ambitions. This is not the man for a clinging vine. Even when he does accomplish intimacy, his familiarity with being alone will remain. His need for space has nothing to do with the quality of his love for you, it's because he is who he is, and *that* is how he loves.

The Clues

Let's look at their story to see what she might have missed in her excitement. Before she even talked to him, there were two possible clues: He had never been married by age thirty-four, and he lived alone, up in the mountains in a fairly isolated setting. These clues in themselves do not have to mean anything at all, but they are worth noting. He *likes* being alone. He is used to it. Remember, what is familiar is very seductive, whether it is good for us or not. Next, he said on the phone, "It is so rare to talk to such a deep woman—it's hard to find people who are true." Right here he is telling her he's been hurt, he doesn't connect often, he doesn't trust easily—not fatal in itself, but certainly a neon sign showing you where he is coming from.

Combining the two, we now know he lives a fairly isolated life and doesn't trust easily. Having this knowledge early on doesn't have to depress you, only alert you to who he *is* instead of who you *wish* he was. Wanting to be "the one who breaks through all that," "the one he can't resist," is a trap. By age thirty-four he probably has met some pretty terrific women, and obviously he has resisted.

Another clue was that he wasn't totally dependable, his passion was not steady and full throttle. This fits right in with the other clues. This is *how* he stays distanced. Next, he calls and says he's coming. It's not about *her* schedule. He doesn't *want* her to change her schedule for him—he doesn't demand much, which usually means he doesn't want to "owe" anything, either. She misses all the clues, completely changes her schedule, picks him up at the airport, brings him home, cooks him dinner, and sleeps with him—all things that feel great but are totally intimate. He enjoys it all in the moment. He knows he still doesn't owe anything because he never asked for anything. He probably genuinely likes her a lot. He sees how great she really is, how warm and giving. There is nothing in their way.

Predictably, he's gone. Suddenly his uncle is the perfect neutralizer, he's off and running. True to form, he avoids any closure. The rushed good-bye is perfect for where he is at. He gets home and misses her—it's safe now, he's far away and back in his own space. He invites her to visit. The time gets close, she's coming. He mines the conversation. She sails right in and hits the mines right on target. He hurts her deeply. She leaves for Mexico. It's truly perfect for him now. He can even rationalize that *she* left him. It wasn't *his* fault—he wanted her to come, but she didn't show up. He meets another girl—younger, less intense. He's on his way. Unless it's someone he feels he's safe from, someone he couldn't love or who couldn't love him, he'll probably act out the pattern all over again. With an older, more up-front woman, the relationship will be quick. With a younger, more naive woman he will go through his typical two-year cycle and end it with another broken heart.

Do's

- Do remember that what you see is what you get.
- Do confront him gently but immediately when you're upset.
- Do gather information and move slowly.
- Do make friends with him first.

Don'ts

- Don't fall in love with potential.
- Don't close yourself off to other opportunities.
- Don't take his need for space personally.
- Don't become a clinging vine.

6

Smothering Mothers' Sons

"Years went by, I watched all my girlfriends get married. Instead of an engagement ring, I got a new set of golf clubs."

The Love Story

He just showed up one day—that's how she always thought of it. One day he was just there and everything was changed forever. Her ordinary life was never again ordinary. She had never known love before—at least not like this. She had been a senior in college at the time, and he had turned up for a sorority charity event. His cousin went to the college, and he was visiting for a weekend. From the start, he was all she wanted. Immediately several of her girlfriends pursued him, but she was too shy. She stood back while they scrambled for his attention. By some miracle, he turned them all down and came after her. It was like a dream after that. They started dating, and by the end of the year they saw only each other. He was with her through all the excitement of her senior year. He came down for all the parties and escorted her everywhere. The only thing that could have made it more perfect was an engagement ring as a graduation present.

She started interviewing for jobs all over the state. If he had asked, she would have gone anywhere to be with him. He never asked. She ended up getting an apartment nearby with a sorority sister and accepting a postgraduate position at the university to stay close to him. He seemed pleased with her choices, and nothing really changed with their relationship. She saw him most weekends, and occasionally they would go away together. She never felt bored with him, he was always so alive. They both enjoyed all the same things, and they mentally challenged each other.

Christmas came, and with it rose her hopes for an engagement ring. He gave her a great tennis racket instead. Her birthday the next summer was the same story: instead of a proposal, she got a new set of golf clubs. She hinted around sometimes, but he never took the bait. In fact, whenever she applied the least bit of pressure, he would pull away and though the sex was good, she somehow felt as though they weren't truly intimate.

After three years, nothing much had changed. They were girlfriend and boyfriend, but their lives remained separate. She had never even met his family. They saw each other the same amount of time each week, and he made it clear he was happy with their relationship as it was. After five years, she had had enough. She still loved him more than anything else in the world and she knew he loved her, but she could not understand why he wouldn't marry her. She had gotten more verbal over the years; now she gave him an ultimatum: "Commit or it's over." It broke her heart when he said he couldn't do it.

They didn't see each other for a month, and then it started up again. But it ended the same way. She wanted what he couldn't give. They stayed apart three months, and then the same thing happened. Finally she decided to seek counseling, hopefully to put an end to this pattern that was killing them. She was stuck, and she knew it.

His Story

His mother was always in his face. He always felt there was no escaping her. One of his earliest memories was the first day of kindergarten, when she wouldn't leave. All of the other mothers dropped off their children and left, but his mother sat at a little desk in the back the entire day. He felt silly—like a little baby; even then he wanted her to go. But no, she became the class mother. Every day she was there, controlling everything. By fourth grade she had gone back to school and gotten her teaching certificate. One year they even put him in her class. Her attention was relentless. She did it out of love, but it overwhelmed him. He was her only child, and she did mothering as she did all things: completely. He felt he had no identity other than as her son. She planned his time, his meals, and the clothes he would wear. She loved Eastern philosophy and insisted they live by it.

The more she came toward him, the more he pulled away. He learned to tune her out and go within himself. Once he got a car, home was history. Later he went away to college and never lived at home again. He dated a lot, but not usually the same girl for very long.

When he met his girlfriend, one reason he was drawn to her was because she didn't chase him. He had room to breathe, to be a man. He liked that a lot. He also liked that she was so independent and athletic. She liked the same sports he did, and they had a lot of fun together. Also, she didn't try to control him or tell him what to do. Everything was perfect until this marriage issue came up and wouldn't go away. She had given him the ultimatum, and he didn't know what to do. He didn't want to lose her; in fact, he could picture being with her forever. But somehow he just couldn't commit to marrying her.

The Intervention

When she came for counseling, she didn't have much hope of saving their relationship. She was set on getting married, and he was determined to be free. They just had not been able to let each other go, and it had been the most painful year of their lives.

He understood her need to be married, and he was as baffled as she was as to why he couldn't do it. He had always assumed he would marry someday, certainly by age thirty-six—which was how old he now was. He said he had tried to talk himself into it—he had even looked at rings one Christmas, but then he was overcome by a terrible feeling of doom and backed off. He acknowledged that he loved her most when she was a bit distant. For him, marriage felt like going to prison.

Initially she had tried to talk him into it. She had tried to explain how wonderful it all could be, but to no avail. Now she was mostly just angry—angry at him and angry at herself as well for letting it go on so long. It was only when she started to realize that his fears really weren't about her that she began to forgive him.

With encouragement, he began to explore his relationship with women and, eventually, with his mother. Then it all began to make sense. His portrait of his mother was overwhelming. Suddenly his cool exterior vanished, and rage and resentment poured forth. He couldn't *stand* his mother, he told her, and he resented her intrusive behavior deeply. His father and mother had divorced when he was very young, and she had never let him know his father. She had controlled that and every other part of his life. He had felt consumed by her. He still felt her presence and still felt incapable of setting boundaries with her.

She always wanted more than he could give. Early on, he had learned to close down as a defense mechanism. He felt safe to come forward only if the other person was backing away. It was the pattern of his life.

Hearing this, she could understand his behavior for the first time ever. It made sense to her now, and she recognized it wasn't her fault—or his. He wasn't keeping anything from her on purpose. In reality, he was operating from a survival mode he had learned long ago. She realized he had overcome a lot to get as far as they had, but she also realized that she needed more. He was not interested in attending counseling, not with her nor alone. He admitted he liked being a bachelor and he wasn't ready to give it up. She began to allow him the space he had always asked for. She decided to begin dating other people. As other relationships filled her life, her need to pressure him was gone. They still saw each other frequently. She enjoyed his company, but was thankful she was no longer dependent on him for her happiness. She was no longer begging for what he couldn't give. In her therapy, she worked on herself. She began to enjoy her newfound sense of independence. A year later, she was offered a promotion at work that required a transfer to another city. She was excited and felt ready to accept it, which she did. She knew now that she was responsible for her own life and her own decisions.

He told her he would come to visit. He was her good friend now and she hoped he always would be. True to form for a distancer, the further she moved away from him romantically the more he ran after her, but they both knew the game now. He had made it clear by his actions that he had no intention of becoming her husband. Once she faced and accepted that, he no longer owned her heart. She knew she would meet a lot of new men in this new position. She was eager to find someone who liked being close and who also wanted to be married. Until then, she was quite happy on her own.

The Clues

The first clue came the first day. All the girls were chasing him; he wanted the one who didn't. A distancer loves space. The next clue comes as she becomes aware that the intimacy is not growing. They have sex, but they remain separated. She *feels* this clue—she can't get inside him. When it's time to make plans after graduation, he doesn't participate in her decision-making regarding her future. She feels on her own, and she is. He does nothing to encourage her to stay nearby. He is showing her he wants no responsibility for her life decisions. He offers her no future.

She decides on her own to stay close by. He's glad but noncommittal, and the years roll by. That is a clue in and of itself. He doesn't want more. He *likes* the distance; he's comfortable with the weekly routine of seeing each other three nights. He feels safe with this arrangement.

Another clue was the fact that he had never introduced her to his family. His mother lived in a nearby
town, but he never discussed her. She knew he saw
her occasionally, but he never discussed their visits
and always seemed angry afterward. If a man hasn't
resolved his family issues, particularly his relationship with his mother, you can be sure this is a clue
that he will have unresolved issues with you as well.
Remember, this was the first woman he ever knew,
and if he didn't feel safe with her, chances are he
won't feel safe with you.

By now it's more than clear that she has a distancer
on her hands and in her heart. There is a lot of pain
connected with loving a distancer, because the closer
you get, the farther he goes away. When you get fed
up and finally pull yourself away, he is knocking
down your door. It's especially frustrating because
often distancers themselves don't know why they do
it. And if you lay down demands, chances are they'll
be gone.

The final clue comes when he just can't marry her,
but by then she's invested over five years of her life,
and the loss is devastating.

Do's

- Do realize that he likes his distance and keep yours.
- Do accept the fact that he's comfortable with an uncommitted relationship.
- Do understand that his not wanting you to meet his family is important.

Don'ts

- Don't waste years of your life thinking he will change.
- Don't get caught up in the game of pursuer/distancer.
- Don't blame yourself for feeling lonely when you're with him.

7

Depressed Mothers' Sons

"He was always upbeat and positive. It got on my nerves sometimes. Then I got sick and he shut me out. When I needed him most, he deserted me."

The Love Story

She had a friend who managed a hotel in the Caribbean and who she had promised for years to visit. Finally she took a two-week vacation in January and headed down to the warm sun. It was marvelous lying on the hot sand, sipping tropical drinks, and reading the spy novels she loved but never had had time to read. One day a film crew arrived at the hotel. They were shooting an episode of *Another World*. She was only vaguely aware of the filming until a handsome blond man came up to her lounge chair and asked her if she would mind being an extra in the next shot. She laughed and said only if she didn't have to move. He told her she looked beautiful just as she was. They shot the scene, and he came back and thanked her. They started chatting about the beauty of the island. He asked if she had been out sailing yet, and she admitted that she had done nothing but lie in the sun.

"Tomorrow?" he asked.

"Sure," she heard herself answer.

He said the shoot was over but that he intended to stay for a few extra days.

The next day was once again picture-perfect. He met her at noon and took her aboard a boat he had hired for the day. Off they went on the crystal blue water. They visited deserted islands nearby and picnicked on pristine beaches. He was thirty-nine, she was thirty-four. They found they had the same taste in music and talked for hours about their favorite performers. Books, movies, all their interests were a perfect fit. Best of all, he also lived in New York City. They knew the same restaurants and had enjoyed the same museums. She even had a close friend who lived on his street. Both of them had been married before, he for ten years ("She couldn't keep up with me," he said of his ex-wife), she for four. All too soon the sun was setting and they were heading back to the hotel. He asked her to dinner, and the glorious day slipped into a perfect evening. When he kissed her good night, she knew they both felt the magic. The next day they played together at the hotel and that evening went into town. He told her he had decided to stay the rest of the week.

Every day after that seemed more perfect than the last. Her girlfriend thought he was great; everyone did. He was funny and smart, not to mention really handsome and fit. When he left it was sad, but they both knew she would be back within a week and they would see each other in the city. The rest of the week was quiet and relaxing. She thought of him a lot and looked forward to going home more than she ever thought she would.

She came home with a mahogany tan and blonder hair. She felt and looked terrific. There was a message on her machine when she got in. "Call me," he said. "I'm waiting for you." He gave her chills. She called him that evening. "Nightcap?" he asked. "I'd love it," she responded. All the magic of the islands was still between them. They laughed and talked for hours. They picked right up where they left off.

Six months later, they were married. He was so much fun and so exciting. He always had several things going all at once, and she wondered when he had time to sleep. Still he made time for her. He took her to all sorts of events and parties. They were always on the go. She could barely keep up with him at times.

The first few months were fine, but then it started to wear on her. They *never* had quiet time together. When she tried to talk to him about deeply personal things, he seemed to tune her out. He didn't want to talk about his own life much either, and he didn't respond to her questions about his family. She knew he had a wide circle of acquaintances. His only interest was in successful, upbeat people. He had no interest in or tolerance for anything he considered "negative." When she got a bad flu one year, he practically ignored her. He couldn't be around sickness, he said—he couldn't even visit friends in the hospital. He said he was intolerant of people who didn't take care of themselves. He was always healthy and happy and he intended to stay that way.

His attitude made her uncomfortable; it seemed so cold and unrealistic. She began to feel like she had to hide anything sad or unpleasant she was feeling. She enjoyed how upbeat and positive he was, but she worried that she could not maintain a similar attitude all the time. It seemed like they could talk about everything except this issue. He was adamant that things be kept positive and up. She loved him and didn't want to lose him, so she did it his way. In spite of this issue, their marriage survived. Over the years she adjusted to the pace, though she could never keep up with it. She told herself nothing was perfect and quit complaining.

Then, when they had been married twenty years something happened that changed their lives forever. She found a lump in her breast, and all the positive attitude in the world wouldn't change that fact. He was stunned when she told him. "You seem so healthy," he said. "How could this happen?" She needed his support, but he closed her out. She went for the biopsy, and it was bad news. They performed a partial mastectomy and advised radiation treatment. She needed him to lean on, but he just wasn't there. He got busier than ever with work. When she expressed her fears and sadness, he changed the subject. He loved her, but her illness stood like a wall between them. She was one of the "sick people" now, and he could not handle it. They came to therapy angry, hurt, confused, and on the verge of breaking up.

His Story

His mother had suffered from bouts of depression her entire life. She told her son that as a girl, she remembered lying in bed sometimes unable to get up and face the day. She married a man who fell in love with her beauty, but after a few years of marriage, he became frustrated and withdrawn with her depressive personality. Their son was the only light in their lives.

He was always laughing and smiling, trying to make their lives brighter and more bearable. He was a smart child and affectionate. He felt badly that his parents seemed so sad and did everything he could to make them happy. He sensed from an early age that his mother could not handle any bad news, so he learned to protect her with his happiness. He would think of jokes and silly pranks to cheer her up. As a child, his greatest pleasure was hearing her laugh, but it seldom happened.

As he got older, he spent a lot of time away from home. He was captain of the football team, star of the school play, and an excellent student. He didn't like being home very much, so he mostly hung out at his friends' homes. He was amazed at how different other families were. His best friend's mother was always laughing and smiling. She was never in bed when they got home from school. She was always busy doing something around the house. He loved it over at their house.

When he came home, it was so different. His mother was in bed a lot. It seemed there was always something bothering her physically, or she would just say she was tired. He loved her so much, yet it made him sad to see her like that. His father wasn't much different, only he seemed sad and angry. They almost never spoke to each other. The son learned to cook his own meals at an early age and to do his own laundry soon after. He still tried to come up with a funny story each day. He would think about it as he walked up the road to his house; a lot of times he just made something up.

Once he left for college, he never wanted to come home to the sadness. Instead, he would find reasons to stay on campus. His parents didn't seem to mind. At first he felt guilty about leaving his mother, but eventually he just blocked it all out. Then he became a busy man on his way up in the world.

The Intervention

Each came to therapy feeling lonely and abandoned by the other. He appeared angry and frustrated. She was brokenhearted. They began by telling a little about themselves, and then each spoke of their reaction to her disease. Somehow, he said, it almost felt like it was her fault, although he knew intellectually that was not true. He admitted he had not been supportive, but said he didn't know why.

She said he was a monster, he had turned on her when she needed him most. She said he had never been there for her, even if she just had a cold or the flu. When her mother had been dying, he wouldn't even go with her to the hospital. She was sick of his "positive" attitude. She had a disease, and she needed to express her negative emotions.

He looked at her helplessly. "What purpose would it serve?" he asked.

To understand better what was happening in their present lives, they went back and explained their respective pasts. She had been raised in a happy, close-knit family, where people shared and resolved their problems together. It soon became clear that his growing up had been very different. He began to describe his depressed mother and distant father. He began to express his anger at the sad home they created for him. He was afraid of sadness, afraid of the depression that cloaked his life as a child. He was determined to be happy—determined to have fun in his life. He had run from that old pain for years, and now her disease had caught him. He was terrified to process any sad feelings, because he believed they would never end. It wasn't *she* he was running from—it was his past. His mother's depression had shadowed his entire life, and his irrational belief was that *any* expression of negativity would result in lifelong depression. He was never able to bring his mother out of it no matter how hard he tried. She might enjoy him for a moment, but she always went back to her pain. That was why he couldn't let his wife lean on him: He was afraid he couldn't help her either, and she, too, would be sad forever.

With that information revealed, she finally understood the man she loved most in the world. She sympathized with his painful childhood and now understood why he had panicked at her illness. Once he began to accept and express his own sadness, he could accept and comfort her. At first he was terrified of the feelings, but gradually, as he began to explore and process all the sadness he had buried, he could accept those feelings as a natural part of life.

He came to recognize that as a child he had been the caretaker of the family. Deep inside he had resented his parents for forcing him into this role. They were supposed to comfort *him* as a child; instead, it had always been the other way around. He began to appreciate the burden he had endured all those years, a burden he was too small to carry. As a grown man, he had been afraid he was still incapable of carrying the burden of life, afraid the result of his efforts would be a repetition of the failure of his childhood. Through therapy he learned about depression—its causes and its course. He began to let go of the guilt that he had failed to rescue his mother from her depression. He began to appreciate the difference between his mother and his wife. His wife was not expecting him to *cure* her, only to *share* her ordeal. As he processed the past, he was able to connect with her in the present. They joined a cancer support group in their community. Eventually they fought the disease together and balanced their sadness and fear with their joy and their faith.

The Clues

Here we have a vacation romance, and they are always tricky. This is one of the unusual cases where the romance actually becomes a marriage back on home ground. Her first clue to who he is, is his extremely high level of activity. He is *always* in motion from the start. Very often, people who cannot stay still are running from something.

Her second clue is in the content of his conversation. It's always about things *outside* himself, never within. Again, this points us in the direction of a man who is not comfortable with his innermost self.

Her next clue comes when she gets the flu and he can't be there for her. He tells her he cannot visit friends in the hospital, either—this is a clue that he is not able to deal with the full spectrum of life. When she asks about his first marriage, his response that "She couldn't keep up with me," is a clue that he prefers to stay on the surface. He doesn't let her in. He's not willing to reveal the deeper issues.

His attitude is another clue—*always* positive. It's great to have an upbeat attitude, but no one can be positive *all* the time unless they are in denial. Denial is a system of defense where we block out what is too painful. Clearly, this is the case with this man. He cannot relate to her sadness and pain because he cannot relate to his own. When she falls seriously ill, the relationship goes into crisis. She needs him desperately, and he needs to escape with equal desperation. They love each other, they have a life together, but they cannot find one another in this very difficult time without dealing with the painful, unexamined past.

Do's

- Do communicate your emotional needs early in the relationship.
- Do learn *why* he's doing what he's doing.
- Do protect your heart with your intelligence.

Don'ts

- Don't tell yourself, "nobody's perfect" and ignore major problems.
- Don't shut off your silent alarm.
- Don't bury your anger.

Part II

The Uncommitted

8

Romantic Mothers' Sons

"He sounded great on the phone, but when we met, it was the worst weekend of my life. I couldn't believe it was even the same person."

The Love Story

She had just moved to a new town. She had accepted the job transfer after ending a dead-end relationship with a married man. She realized she had wasted six years of her life. She was thirty-five now and wanted a family of her own. Her job was going really well, but on the weekends she got lonely. Most of her coworkers were married, and she hadn't made any single friends yet. When one of her friends at work mentioned having a cousin she should meet, she laughed and said, "I'm ready." She told her he was forty-one years old and had spent several years in a relationship with an airline stewardess that was now over. He'd never been married. He was a big, tall Texan whom his family nicknamed "The Prince." He was everyone's favorite. She said he was kind, gentle, funny, and smart and that he owned a restaurant in Dallas that was quite successful. Her friend brought in a picture of him, and he was sweet-looking, just as she described. Next they sent a picture of her to him, inviting him to come visit. Her friend loved being a matchmaker, and before long he called her.

They hit it off right away. She loved his Texas drawl, and they shared the same sense of humor. The first time they talked, it was for two hours. She wondered when he would call again. She didn't have to wonder long: He called her the next day. Before long they were talking every night on the phone. He'd call her when she got in from work, and they would laugh and talk until she had to go to bed. At work she and her friend would share the excitement of this blossoming love affair. After a month or so it felt like he was her boyfriend and she wasn't lonely anymore. He was there for her. They talked about their daily life and shared their weekends on the phone. Letters went back and forth, as well as little gifts. Once he even told her he thought he loved her. He said he often fantasized about marrying her and wondered where their marriage would take place.

His enthusiasm was contagious. She wanted to meet him and felt she couldn't wait another day. He said he wanted to meet her, although it seemed he was more patient than she was. Several times she suggested a weekend meeting anywhere they could arrange it. He said work was really hard to leave right then. Finally he agreed to a weekend in Santa Fe.

She was really excited, then scared. "What if you don't think I'm pretty?" she asked him.

"You're already the most beautiful women I've ever known," he said.

She was packing for Santa Fe when he called. He couldn't leave Dallas that weekend, he said. He just couldn't. Would she come there?

It was a really hard decision. She wanted to meet him on neutral ground. She didn't feel comfortable staying at the home of a man whom she had never really met. On the other hand, she did know his cousin, and she felt like he was her boyfriend. She asked him what it would be like if she came to Dallas. He said there would be a ticket waiting at the airport—all she had to do was get on the plane. When she got off, his would be the first face she would see. He would whisk her away for champagne, and they would dine at the best restaurant in Dallas. Then he would take her home. He would have the guest room all ready for her. The next day he would show her the town. He had tickets to a concert that night, and he wanted her to come to his restaurant. Sunday, after a sumptuous brunch, he would put her on the plane home. She decided to go for it—it sounded great.

A few days later, she was on the way to the airport. She wore a sleek, fabulous dress. Her nails, hair, and makeup were perfect. Walking through the airport, people turned and stared. She knew she looked her best. The flight was smooth, and only as they began their descent into Dallas did she get nervous. She concentrated on that wonderful, familiar voice and told herself she knew him; she just hadn't seen him yet. She got off the plane expecting his face to be there in front of her. It wasn't.

She watched as other people found each other at the gate, and she wondered where he was. Maybe he meant to meet her at the baggage claim, she thought, trying not to let the disappointment take hold. She entered the baggage claim area certain he would rush up to her. He didn't. She was starting to feel more than a little foolish—what was she doing here, anyway? She stood next to the baggage carousel searching the crowd for his face. Curious, unfamiliar faces returned her stare. She got her bag and sat down nearby. She wanted to run, but there was no place to run to at the moment.

Finally she saw him coming toward her. He never looked her in the eyes, and instead of hugging her, he patted her shoulders. Her heart sank—it already felt like it was going to be a long weekend. Still, she tried to relax and stay open. He apologized for being late, saying he went to the wrong terminal. She might have believed him if his ex-girlfriend hadn't been a stewardess for the same airline. She let it slide. They got in his car, and an uncomfortable distance filled the space between them. She tried to be light and fun, but he was wooden. Maybe after the champagne, she thought. Maybe they were just nervous. He pulled up to a restaurant and escorted her to the bar. "What would you like?" he asked. "A glass of wine?" What happened to the champagne? she thought, and she ordered a martini straight up. It was only the second martini she ever had in her life, but it seemed like a good idea. Then her eye caught the dozen red roses with a card on the bar near him. Maybe there was still hope, she thought. Moments later the bartender slid the roses in front of her and said, "Almost forgot your roses." She turned to him murmuring how sweet it was of him, when she saw his face go white. The bartender turned red and said, "Gosh, I'm sorry. I was only kidding." She wished she could disappear or at least wake up from this nightmare.

It never got any better. They had dinner and made small talk, but she couldn't find the man she had fallen in love with on the phone. She went back to his house and tried to settle into the guest room, which he had not gotten ready for her—there wasn't even a bar of soap in her bathroom. The next day he slept until noon and took her to a Chinese restaurant for breakfast. They went to a movie in the afternoon, after which he announced that he had given his concert tickets away. He never brought her to his restaurant. Instead, they had a bran muffin for dinner and he started talking about his ex-girlfriend. She'd had enough. She said she wanted to leave early—he handed her the phone. There was a flight leaving in two hours—she was determined to be on it. On the way to the airport he tried to be a little more friendly; she was ice. She checked in and they told her it was an hour till they boarded. She told him he didn't need to wait. A kiss on the cheek and he was gone.

He called her a few days later and acted like nothing was wrong. He was shocked when she told him it was the worst weekend of her life. He was back into his phone fantasy.

Thank God she wasn't.

His Story

She learned from her coworker, his cousin, that his dad had left when he was born. Actually, his mother kicked his dad out when she was pregnant and she found out about his romance with his secretary. From the start, it was just the two of them, mother and son. He was always her life. His grandparents helped support them, and his mother became a teacher's aide at his school. They were inseparable. As he grew up, he took on the role of her protector. He looked out for his mother and did as much as he could to please her. On holidays they would buy each other special gifts, and all through the year they would surprise each other with little treats. They knew each other so well that one look exchanged between them said it all. She never dated after her husband left. She had no use for men, didn't trust them. Besides, it would have taken her away from her son, and he was what mattered most.

He hardly ever dated, either. When his hormones went crazy, he and the girl next door got together. It was perfect: His needs were met, but he didn't have to change his life at home at all. When he wouldn't marry her after they graduated from high school, she got mad and went off to be a stewardess. At first he was upset, but not upset enough to leave his mother and marry her. After a while he liked the arrangement. She came home once every two weeks or so. It went on that way for years. But then she got tired of waiting for him and met someone else.

He was now forty-one years old and the girl he had been with for years was gone. He was angry and scared. Of course, his mother sympathetically stood by him. She had never trusted the girlfriend much, anyway. He missed the girlfriend and tried to win her back. He even moved into his own condo, trying to convince her he was ready to start a new life. It was too late; she was gone. He kept the condo but still stayed most nights at his mother's house.

Months went by. His cousin called and wanted him to meet her friend from work. She mailed him a picture of her, and he found her to be very pretty. Finally he met her over the phone. Suddenly he started to feel a lot better. He'd go to his condo every night and call her. They had a lot of fun on the phone, and he started to feel really close to her. Somehow, though, he was nervous, very nervous, about actually meeting her.

The Intervention

It's great to meet a man through an introduction from friends, but you're generally better off really meeting him as soon as possible. As we discuss in the clues, until you meet in person, too much fantasy fills the space between you. It's hard not to be disappointed.

Both people create pictures in their minds, and there is no way they can ever be truly accurate. Don't make blind investments with your time; meet him before you give so much of yourself away.

In this scenario, she might have had a phone call or two and either suggested they meet in the near future or just cooled it on the phone until he came to her city to visit his cousin. Had there been no pressure and no expectations, he might have relaxed into it. At least they could have enjoyed each other as friends.

She also might have gotten more information about him in the beginning from his cousin. Knowing about his overly close attachment to his mother and his inability to commit to his last girlfriend might have dimmed some of her enthusiasm for traveling across the country to meet him. Remember, the home team always has the advantage, and she came to bat with two strikes already against her. If he had walked into her life instead of having her invade his life, there might have been enough space for him really to see her. Once she got to Dallas, the game was already over. When he was late, she could have gotten back on a plane, but she had already invested heavily in the fantasy and had to see it through.

The problem is that each disappointment, each painful circumstance, is a bruise on your heart. Some of us get bitter, some get withdrawn, all of us feel and process it in some way. By following clues, *you* get to decide who is worth the risk. Do be gentle with yourself. You want to be in good shape when the right one is standing before you.

The Clues

First clue: Here we have a forty-one-year-old man who has never been married, and she needs to ask "Why?" Asking the right questions and really listening to the answers are everything. That would have led her to the second clue: He lived at home with his mother until he was forty! Clearly there is an attachment there that is beyond the normal mother/son bond. She's falling for a man she's never met without any grasp of the reality she's dealing with. It's easy to say how silly she is, but how many of us haven't gotten caught up in the excitement of a love affair without a clue as to what this man is really all about? Never mind that he's cute, smart, or funny: What is his *history* with women? How does he treat them? What is he looking for? It's so easy to let your heart lead the way—and so dangerous.

Most of us come to relationships with much baggage, especially if we come to them as full adults. You need to examine what's *in* the suitcases, both his and your own. This man couldn't commit for *years*—he's clearly not a good candidate for a husband anytime soon.

The third clue is his hesitation to meet her—to make the relationship real. Phone relationships are tricky: People feel safe on the phone, both with their truths and their fantasies. You can be anybody you want to be on the phone. She's investing a lot of time every evening, week after week, and her fantasies are also growing. I recommend using the phone to *initiate* relationships, not to develop them.

Next, he gets her on his home turf. No matter what the reason, he is now home and safe, and she is vulnerable and at his mercy in a way. By the time her plane touches ground, reality is overwhelming him. He can barely get himself to the airport. Who *is* this woman? To him she has become a major threat to his mother relationship, his old relationship, his entire inner being. He checks out emotionally before he ever gets to meet her.

The next clues are totally obvious. He is late to the airport, no flowers, no champagne, no guest room prepared, no concert tickets, no introduction to work or friends. He's doing everything he can to alienate her, to push her out of his life. He succeeds beautifully. Luckily, she's strong enough to stand up for herself at the end. A woman with low self-esteem might get pulled back into the phone fantasy once she returned home. She might accept his brief apology and start the relationship back up, but it would most likely end in disaster again. He is able to function well on the phone, but crossing over into his real world would probably lead to the same type of rejection.

Do's

- Do explore his history with women.
- Do examine carefully the "baggage" he is bringing into the relationship.
- Do be gentle with yourself.

Don'ts

- Don't live in a fantasy.
- Don't make blind investments with your time.
- Don't let him break your heart more than once.

9

"Perfect" Mothers' Sons

"He was my total dream man, so I hung on for a long time. But after a while, all the fancy dinners and bouquets of roses couldn't make up for the fact that I could never count on him. He was always letting me down."

The Love Story

It was her dream trip to Europe. She and a girlfriend booked Air France to Nice for two weeks of playing in the South of France and Italy. The tiny country of Monaco was their first stop, to attend the Grand Prix. While having lunch at their hotel, a group of men at a nearby table sent over a bottle of wine. There was one man who caught her eye. She guessed he was French. He guessed she was Italian. They both wondered how they would communicate. After lunch the men who sent over the wine joined them for dessert. He quickly took the seat next to her and inquired in Italian, "Where are you from?"

"Los Angeles," she answered.

He laughed and in perfect English said, "Me, too!"

The laughter never seemed to end for them. It turned out he lived a mile away from her in Los Angeles. He, too, was in Monaco for the Grand Prix. They had dinner that night and spent the next day exploring the countryside. He took her with him to view the race, and they drank champagne with the winners. They talked endlessly about their past as well as their dreams for the future. He was twenty-six years old and had never been married, though he had been engaged several times. He came from a wealthy family and talked a lot about his parents, especially his mom. She sounded incredible. She was a successful career woman as well as a super mom. Beautiful, athletic, smart—she was a woman who had and did it all. She had clearly passed a lot on to her son.

He was exquisitely dressed, perfectly groomed, and the ultimate gentleman. He wined and dined her all over France, expressing pride in escorting someone of her accomplishments. She had grown up poor and had to work hard for everything. She had completed college on a scholarship and worked full time while she got her master's degree. Now, at thirty-six, she had a solid career and was financially secure. She hadn't had much time for relationships and was ready now to be swept off her feet.

By the time she left for Italy, they could barely say good-bye. He called her at each hotel in Italy and had roses delivered the first day she came home. They started dating—it was a lot like Europe. Actually, that's exactly what began to be a problem. It was *always* champagne and fancy dinners. He was *always* dressed perfectly and had total grace. It was never just casual. She felt she could not get to the next level with him. They were always on the surface, and she hungered for more. She tried to talk to him about it, but she never got through.

The one thing he was never gracious with was her time. He was always late and often canceled at the last minute. Once he didn't show up at all. She would get angry, but he would always charm her out of it. Sometimes she thought about ending it, but she didn't want to let him go. He was so much fun and so exciting. Even though he was young, he was always teaching her things and showing her new experiences. When he was with her, he made her feel like the only woman in the world for him. They were so close, they communicated so deeply. He was almost the perfect man, but it felt like he was behind glass and she could never break through. It was a glamorous relationship that didn't hold up in the day-to-day, but she loved him too much to let go. One day he didn't show up and he didn't call. She left messages for him, but he never returned her calls. She was heartbroken.

Everyone else seemed so ordinary and uninteresting after him. Six months later, there was his voice on her answering machine. Warm and soft, apologizing for the break in contact, explaining he'd been in Australia on business. She didn't return the call. He called the next day and got her. Before long he had her laughing and agreeing to see him again. They had a marvelous time. She believed him when he said this time it would be different.

Before long the same sort of problems emerged. He couldn't keep his commitments to her, even in the smallest ways. It seemed the better an evening they spent, the more alienating his behavior became.

Finally she broke it off. Months went by; then he called her. This time he said he had come to a realization. She was the only woman he had ever loved. He wanted them to be together forever. He wanted to marry her. He wanted her to have his children. Again, she let herself believe him.

It was the hardest fall of all.

His Story

His parents had met in college. Their love affair was storybook. She was the editor of the school newspaper, he was the captain of the debating team. Both of them were athletic and popular. They were engaged by their senior year and married as they began working on their master's degrees. By the time they received their postgraduate degrees, she was pregnant. He entered the family business. She worked in his office. They bought a beautiful home in Beverly Hills and took trips abroad to furnish it. With the birth of their son, their life was truly idyllic. He was the first grandchild and was doted on from birth.

Every step he took, every word he uttered was greeted with their joy. He was their perfect little boy. By eight years old he was wearing little navy suits and spending time at his parents' office. The entire staff catered to him. He had no idea that his life was unusual.

The family summered in the South of France and skied at Aspen in the winter. He attended the finest prep schools and was at the top of his class. They led a charmed life. From the beginning he was truly his mother's son. She was always there to explain to him, to teach him, to compliment him on his efforts. He watched her run the servants at home and the staff at the office, yet she always had time to read him a story. Of all the mothers who came to school, his was the most beautiful. He was as proud of her as she was of him. She encouraged him to be careful of girls, not to get too involved, not to get tied down, to treat them beautifully but never to lose his head.

He learned that lesson the hard way. He fell in love one summer. He thought for sure his mother would understand and love her, too. He was wrong. She went to public school; he never had. She was not of their faith. His mother insisted he go away that next year to school. He never saw his girlfriend again. After that, he got better at his mother's style of romance. It had hurt too much to be torn between his love for his mother and for a girl. He couldn't take it when he upset his mother. Besides, he didn't feel like he really needed a girlfriend, anyway.

As he got older, his best friends were always couples. The women would all pamper him. They could never figure out why he didn't have a girlfriend of his own, but they loved having him around. He entered the family business and was rewarded handsomely. By twenty-five he had a beach house, a Ferrari, and a BMW. He could be with a different beautiful woman every night, and often he was. He told himself he had not met the "perfect" woman yet. He figured that someday it would all just work out—or maybe he was just meant to be alone.

The Intervention

It's as though she went shopping for groceries at a fast food joint. In other words, don't look for lasting love on a temporary vacation. The idea is to have fun. The chances of finding more than that are slim. It can happen, of course, but you're better off going in with no expectations.

In our love story, she believed in him from the start. She might have had more fun and met more people on her vacation if she had seen him a few times rather than all the time. Instead, she immediately played it all his way. They always did whatever he suggested. It's easier to keep your perspective and hold on to your heart if you create (and stick to) your own schedule. If she had limited her dates with him, she would have been less likely to get so swept away. For her, they became a fantasy couple overnight. Unfortunately, things that start fast tend to end just as quickly.

To have had any chance of getting this guy out of

his old set pattern with women, she would have had to alter his game immediately. He is used to every woman doing what he wants, when he wants. He is used to having his glamorous life-style make up for all the parts of him he cannot or will not give. She would have had to deglamorize him and get the relationship on her terms. When they got back to L.A. she might have invited him for an easy, casual drink at home. If he couldn't allow that sort of intimacy, she would have known a lot more about him. If she had listened to that "funny feeling," that "hungering for more," she might have gotten off the train much earlier. He began to disappoint her, canceling dates, showing up late. If she had not accepted his charming apologies, not been swayed by his roses and other extravagant gestures, she might have faced the reality of his behavior.

Again, time is of the essence. It is a critical element to consider in your relationships. To spend a year or two on the wrong man can be a major mistake. Not only do you endure more pain because the feelings have intensified with time, but also you have also missed out on a year of other people. Especially if you are over thirty and hoping to have a family, why waste the time? Certainly there is something to be said for the experience of it all, but mostly people are damaged by painful relationships, not enriched by them. If you follow the clues, you can cut through the relationships with no future and find the one that's workable and right for you.

This was a man always looking for a first date. In the beginning, that feels great. Every night with him is new and exciting. That is why so many women will fall for him. But in the end, it's a heartbreak for them all. The more perfect she appears to him, the sooner he'll move on. A great woman is a great threat to him. If he had an intimate relationship, not only would he have to face realities about himself (something Mom never made him do), but he would also have to change his life-style. Therefore, the more he can control a woman and the more he is sure he would never marry her, the longer he will let it continue.

Recognize this type of man, early on. If you can enjoy him for what he is, that's fine. But be careful. It's always a temptation to think you're the one who can change him. If you can truly be his friend and not hunger for more, then you're safe. If he himself seeks change and gets help, then, of course, all things are possible. In the meantime, remember: He's like a big, beautiful, poisonous birthday cake—inviting and delicious but, ultimately, deadly.

The Clues

First of all, she met him in the South of France—a playground for the rich and famous. Of course, all things are possible, but vacation romances are notorious. Everybody is away from their normal life. You can enjoy it all, but always try to keep it in perspective, no matter how real it seems. Better to consider it a short-term fling and be surprised if it outlasts your tan. Her first real clue is his revelation about his mom. She just met him, and already he has gone to great lengths explaining his mother's accomplishments. It's great to love your mother, but it's unusual to have her that present that fast. What about other women he has loved?

That leads us to the second clue: He is twenty-six years old and he has never been married, but he has been engaged several times. You need to ask yourself, "What's up?" What happened to those other women? It is amazing what people will reveal if you *just ask*. Most people talk more than they listen. Try to reverse that ratio. She who asks the questions holds the power of the conversation. This man might have readily admitted that no one ever measured up to his mother or that no one ever got along with his mother. He might have said his girlfriend complained about his unreliability or at the last moment he had backed out of the relationship: important information to gather. She might have gotten the whole picture early on by simply asking the right questions.

Next, he always wines and dines her—a lot of fun, but she begins to get a little uncomfortable. *Trust your instincts.* Very often clients tell me, "I had a feeling, but I thought it was crazy." We pick up information on so many levels. Often we *feel* it long before we can determine exactly what is going on. He was stuck on the surface of his life, and though she loved the glamour, it didn't *feel* quite right. She never meets his friends, nor is he interested in meeting hers. He stays unconnected, giving the clue that he may leave at any time.

Then he's undependable. Is he trading on the

glamorous dates? Yet bet! This man is used to getting his way. He may be late, but you're on your way to the best restaurant in town with a handsome man in a red Ferrari. Are you willing to tell him to forget it? Most women aren't, and he is aware of that. His unspoken message is, "I will give you fun, but don't depend on me." If you go, your unspoken reply is, "I will settle for whatever you are willing to give." Remember, everyone has always doted on him and believes he could do no wrong. He still believes it.

As she gets closer to him, he disappears. When a man doesn't return your phone calls, it's always a major clue. Not only does it signal the end of a relationship, but it also tells you *a lot* about the nature of this man. He doesn't even call you to say good-bye. For all of his great manners, he doesn't have the decency to return your call. What he does or doesn't do is driven by only one thing: what *he* wants. How you are feeling is not part of his program.

She lets him break her heart again and again. His old patterns come up every time. The harder she tries to be perfect, the more dangerous she appears to him. In some ways she's a lot like his mother, which means she has strong marriage potential, but his pattern is set. He cannot marry her; he already has his mother, and in a sense is married to his mother's image. Girlfriends who are clearly not anyone he would think of marrying feel the most comfortable to him. He's been living this way for at least ten years, and without professional help there is no indication he is ever going to change.

Annette Annechild

Do's

- Do create and stick to your own schedule.
- Do deglamorize him.
- Do face the reality of his behavior.
- Do pay attention when you're hungering for more.

Don'ts

- Don't believe in him before you really know him.
- Don't put him on a pedestal.
- Don't believe that his glamorous life-style will make up for the heart he won't give.

Part III

The Controllers

10

Critical Mothers' Sons

"I feel like my husband is the school principal, the way he is always chastising me—it seems no matter what I do, I don't do it well enough to suit him."

The Love Story

It was New Year's Eve, which was the only reason she had let her friends drag her to the party. She didn't like parties much, especially big ones. She was shy and easily intimidated by strangers, but they had convinced her she couldn't stay home on such a holiday night. The party was as bad as she expected, and she could hardly wait until midnight so she could leave. At last, midnight arrived. She hugged and kissed her friends and headed for the door.

"Why leave now? The party is just getting started." She turned toward the voice, and she knew she wasn't going anywhere. He was tall and dark, with bright blue eyes.

"I'm not much of a partygoer," she said.

"Then let's go for a walk," he countered.

She laughed and nodded, and out they went walking. When they returned, the party was in full swing. It was the first party she could ever remember really liking. Of course, it was *him* she liked. Neither of them drank, so they sat talking to each other. He made her laugh by critiquing everyone else at the party. He made fun of their clothes or the way they danced or how much they drank. It was all light and silly, and she played along. It was the best New Year's Eve of her life.

He called her the next day, and they went to the park and played in the snow. He told her he was an engineer for an aircraft company. He was forty and had never been married, but he said he wanted to be married someday. He had lived alone since he left for college at age seventeen, except for a roommate his first year in the dorm. He asked her about herself. She told him about her large family, how close they were and how much fun they all had when they got together. She mentioned she had been divorced for three years from a man ten years her senior. But when she said she was forty and worked in an insurance office, he asked her, "Why?"

"It is a good job," she said, feeling a bit defensive. She liked her job. He told her he thought she was a very bright woman and wondered why she didn't want more for herself. He saw he was annoying her, so he backed off and never mentioned it again.

Spring came, and they were officially a couple. They spent all their weekends together, and he left some clothes in her closet. She wanted him in every part of her life. She was excited about him getting to know her friends. She arranged small dinner parties to introduce him to everyone. After their evenings socializing, he proceeded to find fault with each of her friends. He had something negative to say about everyone. It made her uncomfortable, and she found herself defending her friends. Eventually they ended up spending most of their time with only each other. She felt it was just easier that way.

She never met his family because they lived in another state. He met hers, and it was the same old story: He had something negative to say about everyone. No one ever seemed perfect enough for him, no one except her. It struck her that he was great at dishing out criticism, but he couldn't handle receiving it at all. She never mentioned that to him. Instead, she pushed his behavior that bothered her out of her mind.

They married on New Year's Eve, one year after their first meeting. She told herself how kind he was to her, and she knew she felt a strong connection to him. She was sure he truly loved her, and she was a happy bride.

Within the first few months of their marriage, she began to notice a change in him. The criticism he exhibited toward her friends and family suddenly became directed at her. He complained that she didn't keep the house perfectly, she didn't get paid enough at work, she didn't cook very often, she was messy in the bathroom . . . it never seemed to end. He was always complaining about something. The more he criticized, the more mistakes it seemed she made. She felt she had married a correcting, chastising school principal. One day she had had enough. She packed her bags and went to stay with old friends. They encouraged her to seek marital counseling, which, fortunately, she did. Her husband agreed to participate.

His Story

From his earliest memory, she was on him. No matter how well he did something, she seemed to think there was always room for improvement. He felt like she was never satisfied with him or his older brother— but his brother ignored her. He never could. He took her words to heart and always tried harder. His mother loved both her kids, but because of his constant need to please her, he was her favorite. His mother gave up on her husband and older son, but she never let up on him. He isn't sure when it happened, but one day he realized she didn't have to criticize him anymore—he now did it to himself. He was always pushing to be perfect. There was no question in his mind that he wouldn't have succeeded without his mother's constant criticism.

His mother loved her younger son with her whole

heart, and told him he could have the life she never had. Life had disappointed her in many ways, and she had disappointed herself. She had been the brightest student in her drama class—everyone thought she would go far. Instead, she gave up her dream of being an actress in the big city, married a local boy, and had a family. She loved them, but she always had hoped for more. He had felt pressure his entire life to succeed because she counted on his success to make her own life worthwhile. He was always pushing, as though his world would collapse if he stood still. He viewed life as a very difficult task and felt one had to be vigilant and hardworking just to survive; to be successful required even more. He felt alienated from his brother and father, who were more interested in having fun. It was like there were two teams in his family: He and his mother were the taskmasters, and his brother and father were the players. He eventually became more financially successful than this brother, but as he began to talk about his family, he began to wonder who was happier.

The Intervention

When they began therapy they were clearly at odds with each other but had agreed to live together, at least temporarily. To begin, each gave his or her version of their situation. They were like guns pointed at each other, going off again and again.

She complained about his critical nature—how she never felt good enough around him.

He complained that she was careless and haphazard. He described how he wanted their daily life to run.

She said she wanted the freedom to live each day as it came.

As the sessions continued, it became clear that in response to his criticism, his wife had taken a "passive-aggressive" stance—that is, she would never respond directly to his behavior but would instead "get him later." She would not respond to his nagging but would intentionally do things she knew he hated. This covert game had alienated them from each other. As she began to confront each situation more directly, the game had to end. Once she was no longer feeding into his pattern, he had to begin to look at it himself.

In the course of treatment, he started to talk about his mother; he came to recognize how he had internalized her. He had hated her criticism as a child; now he had made his wife the child, and he had become the critical mother. When his anger and depression surfaced, he recognized how pressured and unhappy he had felt for years. He examined the unconscious beliefs that guided him and recognized how afraid he was to ease up on his own rigidity. As he gradually eased up on himself, he was then able to ease up on his wife.

Together they found their sense of humor again. Instead of attacking one another, they could begin to laugh at their differences. He started to enjoy his life, and the happier he became the less rules and rigidity governed him. She continued to work on expressing the inner monologue she had never shared with him.

She began to trust him with the truth, and they found each other as friends again.

They also looked over their daily life and began to negotiate how to structure it. Eventually they came up with a plan they could both live with. When problems arose, it helped her knowing that when he criticized her, it was because he was experiencing fear and self-doubt. Instead of getting caught in the surface events that were merely symptomatic, they began to talk about their underlying feelings.

Then she met his mother. Everything he had said was more than true. But now they were able to laugh together at his mother's constant criticism. They teased her and let it all go. He was thankful he no longer was like her. He loved his new life and his revitalized marriage, *and* his mom.

The Clues

She didn't have to wait long for her first clue. On the evening they met, he immediately begins to make fun of the other guests at the party. She misses that clue because his criticism is not directed at *her*. It actually feels light and fun to her. In effect they are colluding with each other, and everyone else is on the outside.

Her second clue is that he's forty and has never been married. That doesn't necessarily mean something negative in and of itself, but if a man isn't married by forty, you want to explore why.

Her next clue comes when she tells him about her

job and he implies that it's not good enough for her. He hardly knows her, and already he's questioning her work choice. It's a subtle clue, but worth noting.

She didn't get to meet his family, but had she asked about them early on, she might have gotten a clue about his mother's critical nature. When he meets her friends, his critical nature strikes closer to home. It makes her uncomfortable and defensive. Whatever a person is projecting outside the home eventually will show up within the home as well.

In our story, had she been picking up the clues of his critical nature, she wouldn't have been so shocked when he eventually turned it on her. It is not surprising he can not handle criticism that's directed at him; that's actually the core of his problem. He is probably hardest on himself. He is terrified of not being perfect. When he married, she in effect became a part of him—she had to share all his self-criticism. Instead of directly addressing the problem. she acquiesces, and they stop socializing. Certainly, relationships are filled with compromises, and some compromises are healthy. Household chores, finances, restaurant choices—these are all appropriate types of issues to work out with compromise. Certain other things are not. When you begin to compromise yourself, your friends, or your beliefs, eventually you will resent it, and the pendulum will swing the other way. Many marriages are destroyed by people not communicating their desires and objections. Eventually they cannot take it anymore and either explode or turn their anger inward and become distant and depressed.

She needed to call him on his behavior immediately. She needed to let him know she would not tolerate a life filled with negativity and an expectation of perfection from others. Remember, it's much easier to make big changes like this *before* you are married. Very often men will say, "I've been the same way for years—*now* she hates it." It's hard for a man to accept that she hated his behavior all along and only *pretended* it was acceptable. Mixed messages really confuse people. Sometimes you won't know *why* you feel something, just that you do. It is best to express the feeling *and* the lack of self-understanding. This prevents a buildup of an attitude that can be the beginning of a wall between partners. *If you have an inner monologue you don't share with him, you are headed for hurt.*

Do's

- Do confront each situation directly.
- Do share your inner monologue with him.
- Do talk about underlying feelings.
- Do keep your sense of humor.

Don'ts

- Don't pretend to accept behavior that is unacceptable.
- Don't take a passive/aggressive stance.
- Don't get caught up in surface events.

11

Compulsive Mothers' Sons

"He isn't generous or affectionate anymore. He seems more interested in a clean house and his next case than he is in me. I'm sick and tired of how serious and lonely my life has become."

The Love Story

When she got her third speeding ticket, she knew she was in trouble. She had only been going 35 mph, but it was in a 25 mph zone. She had already been to traffic school and was worried about losing her insurance. She contacted a lawyer in town to find out what she needed to do. He had her come in to discuss it, and the moment they saw each other, sparks flew. He asked her a lot of personal questions. She told him she was thirty-three, had never been married, and had worked on and off in her family's clothing business since high school.

By the time he went to court with her, they were dating. He was an exciting man to have a relationship with. He was forty-five years old and had had two brief marriages to "immature, scattered" women. He was powerful, impressive, and very hardworking. Often they didn't have dinner until ten at night because he worked so late. He always called in advance to let her know, though. He was highly organized and responsible in every way. Her last boyfriend had been the opposite, so she really appreciated these qualities in him. The relationship continued throughout the year. On the next Valentine's Day, he proposed. Six months later, they were married. They came back from their honeymoon and began to settle in to married life. She didn't find it all that easy. He was always in motion; she was much more laid back. He wanted the house perfectly clean and every detail of their lives in order. She was much more casual about life. Then his enormous commitment to work began to bother her. He came home most nights after 9 P.M. and left in the morning by 7:00 A.M. Weekends he brought home stacks of legal reading material and plowed through it for hours on end. When he did take time off on the weekend, he insisted on being active—doing chores, cleaning, never relaxing. They didn't make any friends because he was too busy to socialize. In a year's time she had become very unhappy and her life no longer seemed fun and exciting. She realized she was more lonely married than she ever was single. She started to resent his career, and they began to argue a lot. Finally they decided to seek counseling.

His Story

When he thought of his mother, he pictured her cleaning. All day, every day, she worked on their house. She scrubbed floors and tore china closets apart as a daily routine. She never had time for much else. He remembered when he was young, wanting her to play with him. She was always too busy cleaning. She never watched television or read a book. Even if they were driving somewhere on a family vacation, his mother would be busy in the front seat, organizing everything. She would clean out the glove compartment, her pocketbook, and his dad's wallet. Then she would straighten out her appointment book and sort through papers. It never stopped. His dad would make jokes about it, as would all the relatives, but it was accepted as natural and normal. He could remember waking up at three in the morning and hearing her vacuuming.

As he got older, his friends teased him about how he was always busy. He admitted to being a "little like his mother," especially compared to his sister, whom he considered "a slob." His mother never really had spent a lot of time with either of them. He thought she was a great mom—he was just sorry she hadn't spent more time having fun with him when he was a kid.

The Intervention

When they began counseling, it was clear they had forgotten what had attracted them to each other. He complained that she was sloppy and careless and that she had no appreciation for his hard work; all she wanted to do was have fun. She responded by saying he *never* wanted to have fun. He was too busy working constantly. He wasn't generous or affectionate and seemed more interested in a clean house and his next case than he was in her. She was sick and tired of how serious and lonely her life had grown.

As counseling progressed, they began to look at their expectations of marriage and each other. They began to explore what their role models had been and what their childhoods were like. He began to talk about his mother. He laughingly spoke of her cleaning until three in the morning. Gradually he began to explore the depth of his mother's compulsive personality and how it had affected him. He felt best when he was very busy, and he was afraid of unstructured time—it made him nervous and uncomfortable. It was the first time his wife realized it wasn't as simple as him freely choosing work over her. He explained how he felt *compelled* to be busy and that it relaxed him. She began to understand it was not his reaction to *her* but rather his way of coping with life.

She spoke of her upbringing, which had been very different from his. Relaxed and casual, no one was very busy at all. She had been drawn to him because he was so very different from anyone she had ever known.

They looked more deeply at what had attracted them to each other. He talked about her free spirit and sense of humor. She spoke of his dedication and sense of responsibility. They began to understand that neither could change their basic personalities, which were very different. Instead, they needed to focus on the *benefits* of their differences. While it was true he didn't have a great deal of time available to be with her, he did offer her many things. They enjoyed great sex. He was as compulsive about pleasing her sexually as he was about everything else. She loved his sharp intellect, and the time they had together was stimulating. His compulsiveness about a clean house took that burden off her shoulders—she didn't have to clean the house, he preferred doing it himself. For it to work, she would have to reframe how she viewed all the free time this marriage allowed her. She could return to school if she wanted or study languages or dance, all of which had been unfulfilled dreams for her until now. If she didn't mistake his lack of *time* for lack of *interest*, perhaps she could accept his busy schedule.

They began to negotiate their time together. He was willing to commit to being together one weekend day and two early evenings a week. The rest of her time she began to schedule with fun and exciting things. He agreed to pay for her schooling, another benefit of his hard work. Compulsive personalities do not change easily, if at all. The best he could do was offer her a compromise. She accepted his terms, and their marriage transformed. She became much happier as she got involved in her own interests. She no longer sat around waiting for him, feeling angry and disappointed. She made new friends and began to socialize with them. They knew their schedule, and they both accepted it and stuck to it. The marriage went from frustrating cohabitation to a true partnership. Instead of criticism, they began to handle their differences with humor and to accept and love each other—just as they were.

The Clues

Right from the start, she knows he is a very busy man. Her first clue to his driven personality comes when he has to meet her at 10:00 P.M. for their dinner dates. Working late isn't an occasional thing for him, it's his daily routine.

Her next series of clues comes as she observes his life-style. He is highly organized and detail-oriented. His home is spotless, his attention to detail relentless. Instead of considering the downside of this type of personality initially, she simply enjoys the benefits. His hard work has made him financially successful; his home is a pleasure to be in, unlike her last boyfriend's low-rent disaster apartment. She likes his energy and active life-style.

Caught up in the excitement of the relationship, she doesn't consider how differently she lives her life. Even their situation upon meeting reflects who they are. She has three traffic tickets because she's careless; he's a successful lawyer because he is not. She likes the idea of who he is—powerful and successful—but she fails to consider what he will really be like to live with on a daily basis. She had taken at face value his explanation of the demise of his marriages. He had said the women were "immature and scattered." If she had questioned him more thoroughly she may have gathered important information on how *he* functioned as part of a couple.

Do's

- Do understand that he may be very different from you.
- Do focus on the benefits of these differences.
- Do take responsibility for your time alone and have fun with it.
- Do negotiate for what you need.

Don'ts

- Don't sit around waiting for him.
- Don't think you can change his basic personality.
- Don't forget the positives when you see the negatives.
- Don't take his busy life-style personally.

12

Childlike Mothers' Sons

"He treats me like his daughter, instead of his wife. I think it affects our sex life. I no longer have any desire for him."

The Love Story

He watched her as she skated by. She could feel his eyes on her. She swung her leg out and spun around, her arms over her head in a pirouette. She heard him clapping as she glided by. She always felt her best on the ice. The cool, crisp air, the pulsating music, the sensation of flying through the air. She had loved it since she was a child; now she enjoyed introducing her own daughter to the magic of it all. She came off the ice and watched as her daughter practiced with the junior class. He smiled at her across the rink. She smiled back and looked away, suddenly embarrassed. The next thing she knew he was standing beside her. He admired her beautiful daughter and pointed out his nephew, who was an intermediate skater. By the time the classes were over, they were chatting like old friends. He was single, thirty-one, had never been married. He seemed surprised when she told him how she had gone back to school to become an accountant at twenty-eight after her husband had been killed in an accident. He invited her to dinner the next weekend, and she accepted.

He arrived the next Saturday night dressed in a suit with flowers and candy in hand. He had made reservations at the nicest restaurant in town. His manners were impeccable. In fact, she felt a bit silly because he treated her as though she were fragile, while she thought of herself as a rather sturdy tomboy. She enjoyed the attention, though, and found him pleasantly old-fashioned. That was the course of their whole courtship. He treated her with tenderness and respect. Occasionally he went overboard, but after all the stories she heard from her girlfriends about ill-mannered men, she felt lucky. He was also wonderful to her daughter. Her daughter missed having a father. He filled the role willingly and beautifully. He called them his two little princesses, and they both felt pampered like royalty.

When he proposed, somehow it frightened her. She was afraid to move on and end this delightful era of their lives. He assured her it would only get better, but still she hesitated. Their courtship had been a fantasy time. She would leave the pressures of her stressful job behind on the weekend and bask in his love. It was the perfect balance. Now he was telling her she wouldn't have to work anymore. He would take care of her forever. He talked about his own family and how he wanted to create the next generation. She liked his family and she enjoyed being with them, but they were so different from her own. Her mother was an independent, successful career woman, whom her father always treated as an equal. She loved her parents, but hadn't lived near them for many years. His parents believed the wife's place was in the home and the children's place was next door. He convinced her she would get used to it all—what was there not to like? He was offering her a beautiful life. Her friends and family told her the same thing. He was her prince—where could she ever find another man who treated her and her daughter so well?

She pushed her nagging doubts aside. She was just scared, that was all. He was a great man and, of course, she should marry him. So she did. She really didn't want the big wedding his family insisted on, but she went along with it anyway. After all, she told herself, he had never been married, and it wouldn't be fair not to let him have the wedding he wanted. Soon they settled into their own home, less than a mile away from his family.

She had taken a month off from work and was more than ready to get back when her month was up. That was when it all started to go downhill. Her first night home from the office he looked like a lost soul waiting for her return. He complained about coming home to an empty house, with no dinner on the table. He hated that she was tired and wanted to go to bed early. She figured he would get used to her schedule, but he never did. Instead, it only got worse; he constantly nagged at her that she didn't need to work. He seemed insulted that she wanted to earn her own money. It didn't stop there. He didn't consult her about decisions that affected the family. When she did offer an opinion, he smiled condescendingly and did what he thought best. Everything started to annoy her. She used to enjoy his protectiveness; now it drove her crazy. She began to feel like his daughter instead of his wife. It seemed to affect their sex life as well. She no longer felt any desire for him. They both became frustrated and angry. At the suggestion of a good friend, they sought counseling.

His Story

When he or his sister would upset his mom, his father would pull them aside and say, "Don't upset your mother. You'll make her sick. She'll have a nervous breakdown, and it will be *your* fault." He and his sister would feel badly and would become afraid that they would somehow hurt their mother. His mother was the youngest of seven children. She was called "Babe" her entire life. Her family struggled through the Depression, but if there was only enough money for one special toy, it always went to Babe.

Babe was also the one child in the family who never had to work while going to school. She married a neighborhood boy who had just come home from the war.

His dad was hardworking and aggressive and loved his "Babe." He steadily climbed the ladder of success. By the time he was born, they lived in a big house on a quiet street. A few years later, when his sister arrived, there was a new car in the driveway and a boat in the backyard.

Babe enjoyed motherhood, cooking and cleaning and being there every day when her kids came home from school. She saw that as her job, and she did it well. Her husband took care of everything else. He ruled. When her kids complained to her about unfair treatment, she would say, "He's your father—we listen to him."

His father was always pulling him aside and telling him he was the male, so he had to take care of his mother and his sister. In essence, the roles began to change; he became the caretaker, and she remained the "babe."

It seemed that the payoff for him and his father was no housework. His sister had to help his mother all the time. If his father needed something during dinner, Mom jumped up to get it. He figured that was how it was everywhere, and he accepted it. It was all he had ever known.

Annette Annechild

The Intervention

They began therapy feeling that their marriage was a big mistake. He felt as if he didn't have a wife because she didn't stay home, didn't take responsibility for the house, and didn't want to have sex with him anymore. She felt like she was in prison. He seemed to want to take over her life and mold her into someone she was not. She enjoyed cooking but hated his expectation that she do it every night. She had always had a housekeeper; he thought that was ridiculous—wasn't it her *job* to cook and clean? She felt so angry and distant from him, the last thing she wanted was to have sex with him.

They began by looking at what the unspoken expectations had been going into the marriage. She expected she could continue her own life pretty much as it was. He expected she would turn into the wife his mother was. Both were unrealistic dreams. They began to share where their expectations started, which brought them to their families of origin.

She grew up with a working mother who was strong and independent. That was her role model, and that is who she became. He had "Babe." He knew about "women's lib," but he associated it "with masculine-looking, big-mouthed women," not with his beautiful, soft wife. He couldn't understand why she wouldn't *want* to take care of him—it hurt his feelings. She explained she wanted to *love* him, not mother him. They worked toward separating the issue of loving each other from *tasks* they performed for each other. Each made two lists: one list of all the things they were not willing to do; the other list of the things they were willing to do. Then, step by step, they either negotiated how to handle the chores between them or consider having someone else doing them.

Once he recognized that her independence did not mean she loved him less, he was more willing to compromise. When he stopped insisting, she became more willing to nurture him.

Very often, when a child/parent type of communication begins to take root in a relationship, the sexuality is destroyed. We become so vulnerable in sex, it is important to feel safe and to feel equal.

As the relationship grew healthier and the exchange became more adult-to-adult, they were once again able to enjoy each other physically, and their sexuality was reborn. He began to recognize how his mother had very much influenced what he thought a "good woman" was. He also started to explore the downside of his mother's childlike persona. He eventually recognized the benefits of having a wife he didn't have to take care of in a childlike way and who, instead, was a full partner in the marriage.

The Clues

Right from the beginning, it's clear he is an old-fashioned type of man. He brings her flowers, insists on paying for everything, opens doors, and takes charge of the evening. It's so easy to relax into being pampered and taken care of and to forget that there is usually a trade-off. He is used to being in control. He likes it that way. Another clue, had she been watching her own reactions more closely, was when she identified with her daughter as one of the two princesses he took care of. Already she was sensing he treated them in a similar manner, which is exactly what she hated later on.

Next, she didn't heed her own inner voice. *Her* clue was her discomfort when he proposed marriage. Somewhere inside she knew something was wrong. Instead of investigating those feelings, she slips into denial. Unfortunately, those issues we deny, remain, and surface later in our lives. Her next clue is his family. He comes from a tightly knit family with a mother everyone calls "Babe." Clearly, his image of women has been skewed. He's also still single at thirty-one. She needs to know why. Are most women too independent for him? Is he too attached to begin a separate life? She needed to wait, watch, and ask questions. A long engagement might have helped her sort out these issues. He also tells her she won't need to work anymore. She needed to ask, "What if I *want* to?"

All of the clues add up to a man who wants a malleable wife he can pamper and control. He is used to his mother and expects a similar type of woman. Had she heeded the clues, they might have been able to discuss their expectations in an unpressured environment. Instead, they arrived in therapy upset that their marriage was in trouble, with each of them dead set on having his or her way.

Do's

- Do discuss your expectations of marriage before you tie the knot.
- Do examine cultural and social differences.

Don'ts

- Don't sacrifice your sexuality to a child/parent type of interaction.
- Don't get married if you need your friends to tell you how great he is.

Part IV

The Neglected

13

Abusive Mothers' Sons

"Something pulled me like a magnet toward him. I know he felt it, too. It broke my heart each time he went back to his abusive girlfriend. But I could wait—I loved him."

The Love Story

She was a brand-new therapist looking for a job, so when she heard that a position had opened at a drug rehab in a nearby town, she immediately applied. She was forty-six and had been in school for six years. She had been married for ten years and divorced for two. It was time to start a new life, and she was ready for it. She had several interviews and was on her way to the final interview with the owner when she saw him. He was bending over a table reading a newspaper. Something had compelled her to turn her head, and there he was. She could not really even see his face, but there was something about him that pulled her like a magnet toward him. She was surprised at her immediate attraction to him. That wasn't her style. She laughed at herself and headed for the owner's office. She got the job, and he called in the clinical director to meet her. They explained the job was to co-run the adolescent unit. She was to be the "mother" of the unit. Then they brought in her new partner. The door opened and there he was, the man she had seen reading the newspaper. He was over six feet tall, with slicked-back dark hair and sea green eyes that were kind but not really friendly. He welcomed her to the unit. Then he was gone. She could barely speak. She had gotten a great staff position, and her new partner was the first man she had really been attracted to since the divorce. Her new life had clearly begun.

Off she went to work the next day. They were sharing an office as well as a unit, and he helped her settle in. Luckily there was a lot of work to be done, and she immediately immersed herself in it. The kids were demanding and difficult, but the two of them worked together well. He never spoke about his personal life or asked about hers. As she got to know the rest of the staff, she soon found out they were a constant source of information. He was a popular subject. She learned he was forty-seven, divorced and presently involved with a woman who was totally unpredictable. No one could understand their relationship. It became apparent that every woman there had a crush on him. They called him "Miami" because he looked like Don Johnson—only better. He had been at the hospital for two years. Everyone was drawn to him, but nobody knew him.

The months slid by, and as they worked together closely, their unit got better and better. People joked all the time that they were like an old married couple, and the kids teased that they were in love. They were half right: *She* was in love. He was everything she had ever wanted in a man. He was not only dedicated, smart, athletic, and handsome; it was his love for the children that truly won her heart. He understood how confused and lost they were, and he was there for them in every way. Together they watched many of the kids pick up the tools of recovery and start a new life. The unit had become a family, and everyone felt it. Meanwhile, stories about his personal life continued to circulate . . . his girlfriend was impossible, she embarrassed him at social functions and was disliked by everyone. Then one day it was over. He called in and took the morning off, citing a personal emergency. Rumor had it that his girlfriend threw him out of the house in the middle of the night. He showed up for work after lunch and told her the rumor was true. She saw him reading the classifieds, and he left early to see an apartment. She tried not to get excited, but she was thrilled.

Time passed, and they continued to grow closer. Christmas came, and in the spirit of the season her professional front softened and she casually invited him to go on a hike in the nearby mountains after their last group session. At first he seemed excited and said yes. Then he apologized, made up an excuse, and canceled. She did not let her disappointment show. About a week later, he asked her to go on the same hike with him on their day off. She was thrilled! He said he would call over the weekend. He didn't. When she went back to work, she could barely look at him. She worked next to him, but he could tell she was far away. He walked into their office and closed the door.

"What's going on?" he asked.

"You were supposed to call me," she answered.

He seemed surprised. "I thought it was tentative."

"I didn't," she replied. Then it all came pouring out. She began by apologizing to him for inviting him out in the first place, and then she told him the truth. How close she felt to him and how wonderful she thought he was. They worked so closely and they demanded so much honesty from the kids she couldn't be anything but completely honest with him.

He sat down, looked her straight in the eye, and said, "If I wrote down everything I wanted in a woman, you're it."

"Is there a 'but'?" she asked: "Do you mean I'm great, *but* you're just not attracted to me?"

"The opposite", he answered. "You're beautiful."

"So?" she pushed.

"I've just gotten out of a very painful relationship, my pattern is to jump right into another one. I want to do it right this time. I want to take the time to heal."

She could wait, her eyes answered.

She went back to work with a renewed sense of

purpose. He and the kids were like her family, and she nurtured them in every way. She brought in treats for breakfast, and the two of them ate quick lunches and late dinners together almost every day. She didn't date. It seemed impossible to date when she was so full of love for him.

Then one day she heard him on the phone talking about moving. She casually asked him about it. Yes, he was moving, and it was in with his old girlfriend. She got up and walked out of the office. She headed for her car. He caught up with her in the parking lot.

"You never gave us a chance," she said.

"We never had one," he countered. "She was always there."

"But the stories I've heard—the horrible way she treats you. Everyone says she's awful to you. . . ."

"No one really understands her."

She got in her car, but not before the tears came. She drove a few blocks, stopped, and let it all out. For almost a year she had held the hope of him. She knew she had to let it go.

A week later, he eloped.

His Story

She got to know the boy within the man in the hospital-sponsored therapist support group to which they both belonged. Over the months his story slowly crystallized. His earliest experiences were dominated by fear. His mother was married at seventeen and had two kids by twenty. His dad left when he was two years old. He and his sister were too much for his mother to handle alone. There was a string of baby-sitters and boyfriends who passed through his young life. His mother struggled through low-paying jobs and ever-mounting bills. He and his sister learned to block out the screaming that erupted most evenings as his mother's frustration and unhappiness grew. He was the oldest and the boy, so he tried to protect his baby sister. If something spilled, he would take the blame—and the punishment. His mother would yell and shove him. He learned if he didn't say anything and didn't cry, it would be over more quickly. He never told anyone. He didn't want anyone to know that his family wasn't like theirs. The situation went from bad to worse: The shoving went to hitting. It continued until he was eighteen and only stopped because he won a scholarship and went away to school. Still, he loved his mother, and he felt sorry for her. He knew that his father had broken her heart. He saw how the boyfriends who followed disappointed her time and time again. He knew he was the only man who had ever stuck by her, and he knew she loved him for it.

Here is a man who learned to go deep inside at an early age. When the yelling started, he learned to block it out. When the shoving and hitting began, he learned to shut off his feelings. Not wanting to be judged by his peers, he closed them out to protect his family. He learned to make excuses to himself for his mother's behavior, to justify it. She was all he had, so he had to believe she loved him. The abuse became part of the love—he had to accept it to accept her. He prided himself on being the only one who understood her, the only one who stood by her. The pattern was in place, and he repeated it with his choice of a girlfriend. Her outbursts were familiar, her treatment acceptable. No one else could understand why he was with her, but for him it was like coming home.

She came to realize that if she had had a conversation with him early on and learned his background, she could have better understood his choice of a girlfriend. She admitted to herself that he never approached her on a personal level or expressed any interest in changing himself. She also took responsibility for ignoring the fact that, after hearing about his past second-hand, she wanted to give him all the love and kindness she felt he deserved from a woman, *although he never asked for it*. In spite of all she knew as a therapist about change only being able to occur if one truly desires it, she admitted that his changing was her desire. She forgot her training, failing to let her intelligence protect her most fragile part—her heart.

As time passed and she became more objective, she comprehended why a man who appeared to have it all remained in such a negative relationship, and vowed in her mind and heart to give her gifts more wisely.

The Clues

From the moment she first saw him, he was alone. While others sat together laughing and talking in the dining room, he stood alone, reading a newspaper. Next, she is introduced, and though she sees kindness in his eyes, she didn't view him as open and friendly. He says hello and then he is gone. If she was using her head and not only her heart, the first alarm would have gone off. Sure, he's mysterious and handsome, but he's also distant and removed. She begins to hear the stories about his girlfriend. She takes his side. She feels sorry for him, wishes she could take him away from all the hurt. She misses the key point: He's a grown man and he *chose* his girlfriend. No one is forcing him to stay with her. On the contrary, everyone would like to see him leave. He's a sensitive man, he knows that women are attracted and available to him. He's with this woman because he *wants* to be.

Months go by, the work intensifies, she begins to confuse their working relationship with his personal intentions. In the work setting it is easy for him to appreciate and enjoy a giving, loving relationship. It is in his personal life that he is familiar with a different type of intimacy. She doesn't heed his signals; she asks him out. He says yes—thinks about it—and cancels, twice. She pours out her heart. He doesn't take her heart but gives her just a little hope. She misinterprets that as a yes, and her dream world grows stronger. She begins to treat him like a husband. He can handle that intimacy because he's safe behind his desk. He never asks her out, even when he is free. That is a big signal that she misses entirely or rationalizes away. Then she stops dating: the cardinal mistake. She has come to believe her own fantasy. She's in her midforties—she's let an entire year slip away, and she never had a chance. He never changed, never acted out of character. He didn't let anyone know him in the beginning, and he still doesn't. He was comfortable in his abusive relationship, and he stayed in it.

That is an important lesson. People usually continue to do what they have been doing. Change is a difficult thing. People come to therapy seeking change, and still it takes a lot of work and a long time to make small changes. Most people whom *you* want to change, don't usually want to change themselves. Nowhere is it more true than in love; "What you see is what you get."

Do's

- Do take responsibility for your choices.
- Do pay attention to his family history.
- Do use your mind as well as your heart.
- Do give your gifts wisely.
- Do believe you are worthy of a special man.

Don'ts

- Don't think that you are the one who can save him.
- Don't try to be his therapist.
- Don't get bitter; get smart.

14

Absent Mothers' Sons

"Once we moved in together, he seemed to change. He suddenly had a lot of expectations. I think he had a fantasy of what a woman should be instead of an understanding of who I am."

The Love Story

She was twenty-six and had been divorced for two years when she finally felt ready to begin with relationships again. The problem was, she had become completely out of touch with the opposite sex. Her job brought her in contact with mostly women, and a lot of them were single and looking as well. She could not bring herself to go to those awful mixers, and bars were definitely out. Still, she was tired of spending most evenings watching a rented movie and eating dinner alone. She had seen a counselor during the breakup of her marriage and decided it was time to go back and discuss her isolation. Her therapist suggested several possibilities for meeting men. The one she liked best was joining the Sierra Club. She loved the outdoors and hiking. The worst that could happen would be that she got in better shape. She called, sent in her small membership fee, and attended an orientation meeting. The first beginners' hike was that coming Saturday, and she signed up. It was a great afternoon. She met a lot of nice people, though nobody she wanted to date. It didn't matter, though, she had really enjoyed the day.

She continued hiking on the weekends and began meeting a lot of new friends, both male and female. One of them was a man she quickly felt close to. He was warm, but shy. She loved to tease him and watch the laughter fill his eyes. They got to know each other slowly as friends. He was divorced and a few years older than she. They talked about their divorces, totally understanding the pain of ending an entire life and starting another. He said his ex-wife wasn't the woman he had thought she was. He had believed she was sweet and caring when he met her, but she turned into an ambitious, never-satisfied shrew. The marriage hadn't been anything like he pictured. When she left him for another man, he said he was actually relieved.

They commiserated over endless cups of herbal tea. One day she realized she was no longer lonely; months went by, and they got closer. They spent so much time at each other's homes, they started talking about moving in together. One weekend they found a great place and put down a deposit. They were both fearful of marriage, but living together felt right. They survived the move and began to settle into their new lives. That's when she began to feel uncomfortable. He seemed to have a lot of expectations of her. Though they both worked the same hours, he expected her to be in charge of cooking. She liked to cook, but she resented being responsible for every meal they ate. Then he bought her lingerie and expected her to wear it every night when they went to bed. She enjoyed lingerie, but she didn't feel like dressing up in it every night for him. Sometimes she just wanted to wear her flannel nightgown or even a pair of sweats.

When they had their first real argument, he seemed stunned when she raised her voice. He thought it was incredibly unladylike and abrasive. He left and didn't come back until the next day. Then he expected her to apologize and sulked for days when she didn't. Suddenly her life seemed full of rules and regulations that didn't particularly suit her. Her tendency was to run away from her problems, but instead she brought these issues into her therapy.

His Story

He had never known his mother. She died during childbirth. He had carried the weight of that tragic circumstance for as long as he could remember. No one ever said it, but he felt they were thinking that if it wasn't for him, she'd still be alive. He always missed her. He had heard stories about her—from his father, from his older brothers, and from his grandparents. They all said such great things about her. His mother had been a very special woman. Soft and loving, feminine yet full of fun. They said she was a great cook, and they all missed her daily feasts. He would dream about her sometimes, and often pretended she would be there for him when he came home after school. He always pictured her the same way, dressed in the flowing robes his dad said she had loved.

In reality, he didn't know much about women. It was just his brothers, his dad, and himself at home. His grandmother had died when he was ten, and after that he really wasn't close to a female. Instead, his life was filled with sports and the outdoors. When girls started to like him in high school, he felt shy and awkward. He didn't really have a girlfriend until college. He married her when they graduated. It wasn't anything like he had imagined. She wasn't soft and loving, she was aggressive and demanding. He didn't communicate well with her; he closed down and eventually she left him.

The Intervention

She began to explore in therapy how she felt about his expectations. She knew she loved him, but she wasn't happy with their relationship. She didn't want to be the image he had created—it just wasn't her. She began to look at where this image began for him. She asked him questions about his mother. When he told her about his childhood and how he had coped with his mother's absence, she began to understand what was going on. He was still looking to fill that picture in his mind of what a woman was. He had held on to those images for so long, it was only natural he would attach them to her. When she resisted wearing the lingerie or cooking the meals, he felt she didn't love him. When she raised her voice at him, he felt like she hated him.

In a loving and calm manner she began to explain to him what she felt was going on. At first he thought she was crazy. He certainly didn't want her to be his mother. But as they discussed it further, it began to make sense to him. The more he thought about it all, the more sense it made. Everyone had always told him how his mother cooked great meals every day— he had always missed her taking care of him that way. Even the lingerie fit; it was still how he pictured his mother.

Nobody had ever told him whether his mother had a temper, only how sweet and soft-spoken she was. No wonder he couldn't handle feminine anger. Once he became more confident of his girlfriend's love, the more he was able to accept her full range of emotions.

Knowing how much it meant to him and why, she began to cook more often for him. He was so appreciative of it now, she enjoyed it once again. It had been his expectation that had driven her out of the kitchen. The lingerie was the same way. They now laughed when she wore her flannels, and he came to love her in them. Dressing up in lingerie became a treat they both enjoyed.

He later admitted to her how guilty he had felt all his life about his mother's death, and he was gradually able to let it go. He realized he hadn't purposely caused his mother's death; she had chosen to give him life, and he now became motivated to do the most with it he possibly could. Eventually they married, and his wife became his best friend. She now shared his innermost self. Her acceptance of that self helped him to appreciate the woman she truly was.

The Clues

The first clue comes when he's discussing his first marriage. He says his wife "wasn't the woman he had thought she was." What did he think she was like? Was his picture unrealistic? He says he believed she was sweet and caring. Is anybody sweet and caring *all* the time? This would have been an excellent topic to explore with him. When a man talks about an ex-wife or ex-girlfriend, you can learn a lot about his expectations and desires. The important thing is to keep an open mind. Remember, there are two sides to every story. If you jump on his bandwagon, chances are you will get to learn less. Keep in mind, she probably loved him, too. She faced the same situation with him as you do now. Instead of viewing her as the evil enemy, try taking her side to balance the information as much as possible.

When they moved in together, the clues started coming quickly. He has a fairly fixed image of what a woman should be. Clearly, he believes a woman provides the daily nourishment. He also believes women should always look a certain way, at least when they go to bed. He would like to see her dressed like a feminine doll every night. In essence, he is trying to re-create the only image of a woman he has ever known.

Next, when they have their first real argument, he cannot take it when she expresses herself in an angry way. Again, he believes a woman should be a certain way. Her healthy expression of anger to him is unladylike and unacceptable.

All of these clues add up to a man who has a fantasy of what a woman should be, instead of an understanding of who his woman is. The clue to look for in yourself is that feeling of discomfort. The trap in a situation like this is to try to *become* the fantasy. You deserve to be known and loved as you are, not as he wants you to be.

Do's

- Do explore where his image of a woman started.
- Do believe in who you are.

Don'ts

- Don't try to become his fantasy.
- Don't believe you're not good enough.

15

Mothers Who Abandon Their Sons

"The closer we got, the more possessive he became. Every good time we had was followed by a fight over something ridiculous he was jealous about."

The Love Story

It was early one Saturday morning when she heard a knock at her door. She threw on her robe and stumbled sleepily toward the door. She looked through the peephole and saw an attractive man looking back at her. "Can I help you?" she asked through the closed door. "I am so sorry to disturb you," he replied. "I'm moving into the apartment beneath you and I wondered if you would call the moving company for me; they are over two hours late." "Sure," she answered. She called, and they told her they were on their way. Before going down to let him know, she jumped in the shower, brushed her teeth, and combed her hair. She laughed at herself for being excited about this guy—he was her new neighbor—no way she could date him, but he sure was good-looking. She went down to meet him, and he was friendly and warm. He had just been transferred into town and did not know a soul. She invited him to a little party she was having the next day. Just to be friendly, she told herself; besides, most of their neighbors would be there.

The party was in full swing when she saw him next. The door opened, and there he was. Only this time he was all dressed up and holding a beautiful bouquet of flowers.

"For you," he said. "Thanks for all the help—I really appreciate it." This man excited her—there was no doubt about it. Not only was he good-looking, there also was a certain feeling about him. Something in his manner was vulnerable, and it drew her right in. He stayed after the other guests had left, and that was the beginning of it all. At first they talked about how they could only be friends—because they lived so close to each other. After about a month, it was clear that the chemistry between them was too passionate for friendship. Soon they were inseparable. They ate dinner together every night and played together every weekend. He was always inviting her someplace, and she always accepted. She loved the feeling that he didn't want her out of his sight. Six months later, when a larger apartment became available in the building, it seemed perfect to move in together. As they settled in to their new place, she realized he didn't have any photographs of friends or family. It then dawned on her how little she knew about his past. She had asked him questions about his family, but he never really answered them. He wanted to know her age (twenty-seven), but he was reluctant to tell her his (thirty-three). She never could get him to talk about what broke up his first marriage.

He seemed to change after they moved in together. He was still fun, considerate, and loving, but he was also extremely possessive and suspicious. Every time she went out with her girlfriends, he would become distant when she came home. If he did speak to her, he was often sarcastic. If they went to a party and she spoke to another man, he accused her of planning an affair. His behavior truly shocked her. When these fights occurred he became so mean. She didn't know how to respond to him. She had no interest in other men, but he was driving her crazy. Months went by, and it only got worse. The closer they got, the more possessive he became. It seemed that after they had a particularly good time together, he would go crazy over some imagined indiscretion on her part. One day she came home and caught him rummaging through her briefcase. He told her he had to know if there were other men in her life. It was the last straw. She realized this man needed help. She told him if he didn't get help, she would leave him.

Annette Annechild

His Story

What he remembered most about his mother was her scent. She always smelled so good to him—so sweet and fresh. He remembered, too, that she would sing to him and stroke his hair at night when she put him to bed. They sounded like sad songs to him, but he loved them because she sang them just for him. These good memories were overwhelmed, however, by his worst memory: the day he realized she was gone. At first, his father had told him and his sister that his mother was on vacation, but after several weeks he told them the truth. His mother had fallen in love with another man and had run away with him to another country. He was ten years old when she left, and not until he was thirty did he see her again. He had heard from his grandmother that she was living in Italy, and when he went there on vacation with his first wife, he decided to try to find her.

It was not the emotional reunion he expected. They were strangers. They tried to relax and communicate, but when she asked him how he'd been, he could only shake his head and murmur that it had been a long twenty years without her. Then he stood up abruptly and left. He could never forgive her, and she hadn't asked him to try. His wife tried to talk to him about it, but he felt he could never really trust her. He was always wondering who she would meet, who would take her away from him. It was a self-fulfilling prophecy. One day she told him it was over and within a few months had moved in with one of his colleagues.

All the pain of his mother leaving seemed to become resurrected as he struggled through the divorce. She said he drove her away with his jealousy; maybe she was right. He didn't date for a full year. He couldn't bear the thought of getting close and losing again. Then he requested a transfer and moved to a new city. He fell in love with the girl upstairs, and even though he was scared, it all just happened. Now he was afraid of loving again, and he was angry that women always let him down.

The Intervention

He came into therapy distraught and unsure if he even believed in the therapeutic process. He was there only because his girlfriend said she would leave him if he did not seek professional help. Initially he resisted answering any questions about his past and felt it didn't affect his current situation. It was suggested to him that he might be more willing to work in couple therapy, so he asked his girlfriend to attend the next ten sessions. She talked freely about his possessiveness and jealous outbursts, which he didn't deny. Slowly he began to open up. As one of their homework assignments they were asked to write a letter to their opposite-sex parent and read it aloud in the next session. When he read his letter, which told the story of his mother's abandonment, he started to cry. Soon sobs racked his entire body. The years seemed to slip away, and at last the ten-year-old boy emerged. The old pain surfaced, and he began to release it. His girlfriend comforted him and began to understand where all the jealousy was born.

From that night on, they were on the same team. He came back to his individual therapy with new insight and a willingness to work. He began to explore that devastating period of his life and to examine how he had tried to cope with it. When he got to his first marriage he began to recognize how he had set himself up and pushed his wife out of his life. He recognized his pattern: The better things got with a partner, the more terrified he became of losing her, so he then alienated her in an attempt to control her abandonment. His mother's sudden departure had caused him to lose faith that anything could remain constant. He began to realize that for all of the years since she had left, some part of him had been blaming himself. His ten-year-old mind had believed that if he had just been better, been more, she would have stayed with him. It wasn't his father he felt she left, it was *him*.

He had been so devastated by the loss of her, he had shut down emotionally. In his life, love equaled pain. As he worked through these old feelings, he was free to begin again. He began to believe that his wife truly loved him and had no desire to leave him. When there were occasional flare-ups of insecurity and suspicion, they were able to examine the situation logically and calmly; first in therapy and then on their own.

The Clues

Her first clue came when he doesn't appear to have any connections to friends or family. It's as though his life began the day he met her. Then he is reluctant to answer her questions about his past. A person who has integrated his past is free to talk about it. A runner is not. If the emotions aren't processed, it is extremely uncomfortable to be questioned about the past. Those old feelings are still alive, and with the slightest provocation, they may come to the surface and be redirected at you. Her next clue is his pace: He fills every corner of her life immediately, and she lets him do it. There is no balance, no true integration of her into an already full life; instead, immediately, she *is* his life.

The clues were in front of her: This is a man with a big empty space inside. She needed to gather information about that space *before* she filled it with her life. In this case she jumped into a live-in situation that closely resembled the two most painful experiences of his life. No wonder his old behavior came rushing back. Of course he's going to expect her to disappoint him—to abandon him, once again in his life. So he tries to protect himself with his jealousy and his rage. He loves her, but he is in a survival mode. In counseling, he began to realize that survival was an old issue for him and that her love could help heal the hurt of that early abandonment.

Do's

- Do pay attention if he is disconnected from family and friends.
- Do use caution if he overwhelms your life.
- Do have compassion for his difficult past.

Don'ts

- Don't let his jealousy make you feel guilty.
- Don't close down your true self to please him.

Part V

The
Overwhelmed

16

Overprotective Mothers' Sons

"Before I was married, I was a ski instructor and a lifeguard. Now I'm trapped at home with a man who doesn't want to do anything but watch TV. He treats me like his caretaker and overprotects our baby—just like his mother."

The Love Story

They met in Colorado during the ski season. It was his first ski trip, at age thirty-six. She was twenty-nine and had been skiing all her life. She was his instructor, and from the first lesson they had a lot of fun. She teased him about his beginner's fears and coaxed him down the mountain. His absolute delight at each little success made him her favorite student. Right away, he was her favorite date. When his two-week vacation ended, he headed back to his teaching job in a town about two hours away. She wondered if she would ever see him again. The next weekend, he was back, this time with his own ski equipment. He wanted to become a real skier—no more rentals for him. That was how the whole season went. He would come up most weekends, and they would ski by day and party by night.

She was younger and more adventurous than he. She kept him trying new experiences. He had never snowmobiled or even ice-skated before. That was amazing to her. She had grown up in the mountains with an athletic, outdoorsy family. Spring came, and he invited her down the mountain and introduced her to his life.

She wasn't exactly sure what she expected, but it wasn't anything like she thought it would be. He lived in a small ranch-style house that was decorated like a little old man lived there. She laughed to herself as she glanced around. Little doilies were under each lamp. There was a La-Z-Boy chair in front of the TV set and a little dish of hard candies on the oak coffee table. Everything just seemed so old and sedate, not at all as she saw her handsome boyfriend. He worked practically across the street, at the junior high school. He took her over and showed her his classroom. He was a math teacher.

When she asked him if he liked working there, he answered, "Not really."

"Why do you stay?" she asked.

He had seven years invested at the school, he told her, and he was looking forward to tenure. She wanted to ask him why he wanted tenure at a job he didn't like, but something stopped her. He seemed different off the mountain, less fun and more serious. It wasn't until they were in bed that night that she really felt comfortable with him again.

Two weeks later, he came back up to see her. This time he brought an engagement ring. She accepted the ring, and they had a great time celebrating. She let his life down the mountain become a distant memory. It wasn't until she met his mother a few weekends later that those uneasy feelings returned. She watched his mother hover over him. They could barely get through a meal without his mother jumping up five or six times to get him something or make something better for him. His mother seemed to know every detail of his life, and she was constantly cautioning him about everything. His mother told her she hated the idea of them skiing and wished they would both stop. He got angry at his mother when she cautioned him about skiing.

She was glad when dinner was over and they could make their excuses and leave. He was quiet all the way home. His mother offered to help plan the wedding, but as it was at her parents' house up in the mountains, it was easy to decline her help.

Soon they were married and moved into their own little house, which she decorated in a bright, simple way. Everything went pretty well the first year. They took lots of trips and had a lot of fun. Then she got pregnant, and subtly things began to change. He didn't want to go on trips anymore. He said they needed to save money, and he was worried about the baby—so skiing was out. He didn't want to eat out much anymore either, although they had eaten out frequently before her pregnancy. She found herself very pregnant and very lonely. She was used to the excitement of people and places. It was the first winter of her life that she spent indoors.

She got tired after all day with the baby and making dinner, and she would fall asleep at eight o'clock while he was still watching television. When she tried to talk to him about her unhappiness, he would lose patience with her. He told her that life was no joy ride and she needed to grow up. She loved their baby and she loved her husband, but she hated her life. To make it worse, his mother hovered over them. She was always stopping by or wanting them to come to dinner with the baby and was continually warning them about some imagined threat to their child. She'd leave these family dinners so nervous, she didn't expect her baby to make it through the night. Finally she couldn't take it anymore. She thought about leaving him but didn't really know how. She decided to find a therapist instead.

His Story

His mother was the oldest of four sisters. After the death of her own mother when she was twelve, she took over raising her siblings, while her father worked long hours in a factory. Life was hard, and they made it through by watching out for each other and being careful. She met her husband shortly after

World War II. She thought he was handsome and brave, and before long she was married and pregnant. By the time the baby came, they were quarreling a lot. He wanted to take chances; she was too ɔfraid. He took their savings and invested it against her will, in his own company. When the company failed, so did the marriage. She went back with her baby to her father's house, and that's where her son grew up.

She was always telling him about all the hazards of life. When other kids went roller skating, she was afraid he would break his leg and wouldn't let him go. She discouraged him from playing school sports and got him to join the band instead. Field trips were out unless she chaperoned. When everyone got their driver's licenses at sixteen, she made him wait until he was eighteen. He had a lot of mixed feelings about his mother It was true that she had dedicated her life to him, and he appreciated that, but sometimes he wondered who he might have been without her. It was she who got him to major in education; he wanted more than anything to be an oceanographer. Then again, he did own his own house by twenty-nine years old and had a steady job with benefits; he had to thank her for all that. When he went skiing that first time it was a big breakthrough for him. He was terrified, but he did it anyway. The more his mother tried to talk him out of the trip, the more he wanted to go. Then to have this beautiful ski instructor fall in love with him—he felt like a new man. She was young and exciting, and unlike himself, she wasn't afraid of anything. He felt so different on those ski trips, so free. Life was fun and full, and for a while he wasn't afraid of anything.

The Intervention

She came into therapy alone, because he refused to come with her. He didn't believe in therapy, he said, and he really didn't see why she needed it anyway. She should feel safe and secure with a nice home and car and a full refrigerator. Meanwhile, she was totally depressed and felt she could barely go on. As she told her story, it became clear that she had given up her life and taken on his life. She no longer skied or swam and no longer kept in contact with her old friends. With therapy, little by little she claimed back her life. She started taking classes at a nearby college and got back in touch with old friends. She convinced him to leave the baby with a sitter for a weekend, and they went skiing again for the first time in years. It reminded them both of where they had started together, and even he had to admit they had gotten lost somehow.

As she became happier, he became more open to therapy and began attending sessions with her. They worked on the marriage, and then one day he opened up about his mother. Out came the rage and resentment he had buried for over thirty years. Then came the tears. He gradually began to separate what were his own beliefs and what were his mother's. He got in touch with the fear he had known since childhood and the resentment toward his mother that had accompanied it. As he cleared out the wreckage of past emotions, he began to relate to his wife once again as the woman with whom he had fallen in love. He transferred to a school in the mountains where they had enjoyed so much together. She began working part time as a ski instructor once again, and their child learned to ski soon after he learned to walk. They still saw his mother fairly often, but once they were a team it was *their* energy and beliefs that guided their times together. One of these days they hope to get *her* on skis!

The Clues

First of all, she met him on *his* vacation—that is even more dangerous than your *both* being on vacation. She is in her everyday life; he is not. She is being herself; he can be whomever he wants to be— temporarily. It is difficult to get a clear picture of someone while that person is on vacation. When she enters into his environment, the clues are everywhere. He lives in a conservative home that she can't relate to at all. He doesn't like his job, but stays with it for security purposes. He's thirty-six, but he's living like an old man. She's twenty-nine, but she has chosen to live more like a kid. She's a ski instructor at a mountain resort and a lifeguard at a beach in the summer. If she was willing to see it, she'd recognize the vast differences in their life choices. The next series of clues comes when she meets his mother. His mother is afraid of everything and negative as well. She dotes on him, which he accepts, but he has an attitude toward her. Clearly there is unfinished business here that will spill over into his female relationships.

She shuts her eyes to all this and ignores the gnawing feeling that is telling her something is wrong. Ignoring that feeling is always a mistake. It *always* pays to stop to consider *what* it is you are sensing. Better to face it now than have it loom up later. She gives up her life and joins his life. He no longer escapes into her world; she is now trapped in his. Suddenly it seems to her that he has become the little old man that his first house reminded her of. He doesn't want to go out, treats her like his caretaker, and overprotects their baby—just like his mother.

Do's

- Do keep in mind who you were before you met him.
- Do keep up your outside interests and hobbies.

Don'ts

- Don't believe him when he tells you that you "should" be happy.
- Don't ignore the gnawing feeling that something is wrong.
- Don't give up your own life and take on his life.

17

Peacemakers' Sons

"Once we lost the baby, everything changed. I was depressed for months. Eventually I started to live again, but the one person I couldn't seem to reconnect with was my husband."

The Love Story

They met one winter at the zoo. She loved to take her fourth-graders there for field trips. She met him when she called the zoo to arrange the day. They hit it off immediately on the phone, and he suggested turning their field trip into an article for the local paper. The kids thought it was a great idea, and on that wintry day, all bundled up, they arrived for their visit to the zoo. He was there to welcome them personally and introduce them to the reporter and photographer. He wasn't really handsome, but something about him was very attractive. They had a wonderful day visiting the animals, posing for pictures, and talking to the reporter. He smiled easily, and his eyes took her in and held her. By the end of the day he had asked if he could take her to dinner. They had a great time. He called her the next day, and they went out again the next night and had another terrific evening. He was genuinely interested in the kids and was as excited as she was about the upcoming article. He was thirty-seven, the same age as she, and lived less than a mile away. He had worked at the zoo for ten years and loved his job. He had been married once, just out of high school, but it had lasted only a year.

By the time the article came out, they felt like old friends. They had the same interests and ideas on living. They were both upbeat, optimistic people who were active and hardworking. They seemed to fit like a hand in a glove. When the article came out, he came to visit her class. The kids loved him. He sent them all candy the next day, and they loved him even more. She was beginning to feel the same way herself. Within a few months they were talking about being together forever. A few months later, he proposed.

Theirs was a fantastic wedding, held on the grounds of the zoo. They honeymooned in Tahiti and came back to their new home together. Life felt ideal to them both. They wanted children and were ecstatic when she immediately became pregnant. It was a joyous pregnancy. They took birth classes and totally enjoyed the entire experience. She had an easy pregnancy—no morning sickness at all. In fact, she was in the gym right up until delivery.

Then everything came crashing down: the baby was born dead. Suddenly there was no child. On top of that, it had been a torturous delivery, and the doctor didn't think she would be able to have any more children. All their dreams came to a complete halt. They were devastated. Weeks passed, then months. He began to live again; she could not. Her sadness only increased as time went on. She refused to return to her classroom. On many days she refused to get out of bed. He would come home from work and find her where he left her nine hours before. He repeatedly tried to encourage her to begin to live again, but she heard it only as criticism and responded harshly. So he stopped trying and withdrew into his own world. He was passed over for a promotion and did not share his confusion and disappointment with her.

After six months there was no improvement. Her doctor recommended therapy, and she consented to see someone. Eventually therapy did help her depression. She began to work through her great disappointment and to begin to get in touch with her anger. She started at least getting out of bed in the mornings. Within a few months, she returned to work. She started to make friends again and reconnect with old ones. The one person she couldn't seem to reconnect with was her husband.

He got on her nerves a lot, especially when he complained about her going out with her girlfriends. One night they really got into it and she yelled at him and told him to leave her alone. If they couldn't be parents, she could at least enjoy the freedom to be with her friends. Who were these people who screamed and slammed doors? What had happened to their marriage? He confronted her when she got home the next night: Things had to change, or he was leaving her.

His Story

He had never heard his mother yell at anybody, and certainly not at his father. No one was allowed to upset the household. No matter what was going on, you were expected not to raise your voice. He never did. His mother worked hard at keeping the peace. She was the negotiator in the family and the cheer-leader. She wanted everything to work just right, and she tried so hard, it often did. She was "the fixer," and the whole family knew it. Dad brought home the money, but Mom ran the house.

He was shocked when he went to visit a friend of his from college. His family was loud and conten-tious. They all seemed out of control to him, but his friend said it didn't mean anything—that's just how they were. He couldn't imagine what it would be like just to let go and express whatever you felt. Most of the time he didn't really know how he felt. He figured he felt good, the rest of his family always seemed to, and no one ever talked about feelings anyway.

The Intervention

As she began to come out of her depression, her relationship with her husband grew steadily worse. She felt constantly angry toward him, but she was not sure why. He felt out of control, terribly sad, and said that if things did not improve in his marriage, he would not be able to take it anymore. She brought him into therapy, and they committed to spend at least ten weeks in marriage counseling.

He was clearly a man "in crisis." He could not sleep and was not eating well. He felt lost and abandoned. When asked about his past, he explained that he had never felt anything like this before. He had a happy childhood and a stable, enjoyable bachelorhood. Never before in his life had he felt such torment, and that was the key: He had no coping skills because he had never dealt with adversity. He began to describe his childhood in more detail. He explained how his mother took care of everything. There was no screaming and yelling or unsolvable problems. There was quiet and calm; his mother saw to that. He had a younger brother who was very different from himself. Although he described himself as very much his mother's son, his younger brother still lived at home at age thirty. His mother took care of him and he always seemed to need her for something.

He, instead, had been quite independent from an early age. He recognized he was a lot like his mother, always taking care of everything and everybody. Slowly he began to recognize how that affected him on deeper levels. Eventually he connected it to his current situation. This year, for the first time in his life, he was presented with situations that were unfixable. Losing the baby had been a nightmare for them both. Not being able to fix it had driven him crazy. To watch his wife depressed day after day and not to be able to fix it was incredibly painful for him. When he didn't get the promotion, it was another blow. The job went to another man, and there was nothing he could do about it. The final blow came when his wife began to recover but was angry with him all the time. He had waited patiently for her to come out of the depression and to be with him. Instead, she wanted only her friends. She had nothing but criticism and anger for him.

She began to understand what he was going through, but still she felt angry at him. Slowly she began to recognize that she had wanted him to "fix" it as much as he wanted to be able to. He had fixed everything else for her up to that point. She had come to depend on him to correct all that went wrong, and now she was angry that he couldn't.

She also realized that since they had met she had stifled her negative feelings. She had grown up in a very verbal, expressive family. From the start she had sensed it was not okay to express herself fully with him, and she never did, especially her anger. When she began to get in touch with that suppressed anger, it came out directed at him. Coupled with her anger at the world for losing her baby, it had grown into a rage that threatened to consume her.

They joined a therapy group whose focus was

mourning. There they were safely able to vent and process their frustration, anger, and sadness. When they lost the baby, they had lost each other, so they began to try to find one another again in marital therapy. As he became able to express his emotions, she began to feel close to him again. During the previous year, when he could not fix everything in his usual manner, he had become confused and had closed down. Unfamiliar with the expression of emotion, he had pushed his emotions down and had become cold and distant. As he expressed his great sadness and anger over losing his child, he was free to feel and love once again. When she saw the expression of his pain, her heart opened to him once more. Together they worked on communication skills and began making plans as a team. Their greatest dream came true when they found out she was pregnant again. They felt stronger and more ready than ever to be good parents.

The Clues

Perhaps the only clue to a man like this comes when a problem arises that he cannot fix. Until that point, everything sails along incredibly well. Like his mother, this man is a "fixer." In a relationship, that initially feels great, he is attentive, giving, and aware, if something is wrong, he sets out to correct it and usually does. He is familiar with a life process where things run smoothly.

Your first indication of his inner dynamics might occur during an argument. He will not be comfortable with any overt expression of anger. Remember, at his house no one did that sort of thing. Because he never had to deal with that type of situation, he is now ill equipped to do so. Our pain as well as our pleasure form us. Negative situations force us to develop coping skills. If a mother constantly smoothes out difficult situations, chances are her children will not develop their own skills in this area. Once again, this type of mother comes from love, but it is a love out of balance. By not taking care of herself and instead focusing all her energy toward fixing her family, she has created children who either continue to depend on her to keep fixing things or become "fixers" themselves.

Do's

- Do allow yourself to mourn your losses.
- Do concentrate on being a team.
- Do learn to vent frustrations and anger safely.

Don'ts

- Don't depend on him to correct all that is wrong in your life.
- Don't bury your anger.

18

Anxious Mothers' Sons

"I've never been afraid of much, but being with him has made me begin to question myself. Suddenly it seems this marriage is going to be too careful and way too serious."

The Love Story

It was her first Thanksgiving holiday on the East Coast. She had always really enjoyed being home with her family in California on the holidays, but this year it just wasn't possible. She was relieved when a girlfriend at work said she was having a holiday feast for out-of-towners. She had had visions of eating a tuna sandwich in her apartment alone on Thanksgiving. This was not going to be a traditional holiday, but it sounded like a lot of fun.

There was fourteen single people coming, each bringing their favorite holiday dish and a bottle of great champagne. When she arrived, the party had already begun. There was music and laughter and homemade dishes from every ethnic background. They went around the table, and each person told a little about themselves and what holidays at home were like. She was immediately drawn to a southern man who told a funny story about his mother. He said she was always so worried about undercooking the turkey that every year she overcooked it till it fell off the bones and nobody would eat it. The only reason he wasn't with his parents this year was that they had won a cruise and were away. She was glad he was seated next to her. They got to know each other during dinner. He was thirty-two years old and like her had never been married, and worked in his family's business, although he talked about wanting to be a writer. When she asked why he didn't have a go at it he replied, "No guts—no glory." He was such a good storyteller, she was sure he could write if he gave himself the chance. She had always been a big believer in following one's dreams.

By the time the day ended, he had asked her out to the movies the next day. She went home walking on a cloud. It had been a wonderful day, and she had a date with a special man tomorrow.

They discovered they loved the same movies and ended up seeing two in a row. They went back to her place afterward, and she whipped up a little pasta dinner for them. It had been another great day. He lived in the same building as his family and he invited her over for Sunday dinner. She accepted, but felt nervous about it all the next day. She didn't need to worry; it was another wonderful day with him. His family was warm and loving and treated her like an old friend. His mother laid out an incredible spread of what seemed like everyone's favorites. She worried about every little detail and jumped up and down from the table trying to make it perfect. She wished his mother could just relax and enjoy it, but she couldn't. But it didn't seem to bother anyone else; she figured they were used to it.

He was her first born and only son, and she was clearly very close to him. Over dinner she seemed to ask him a lot of questions about all the different parts of his life. She cautioned him about everything. He had a younger sister everyone said was the wild one in the family. She lived in California and was trying to make it as an actress.

When he took her home that night, he kissed her and told her it had been the best holiday weekend of his life. He seemed upset when she told him she'd be out of town all week on business. He said he was afraid of flying and thought it was unsafe. She teased him and said she had been flying for more than thirty-two years, and besides she'd be gone for only a week. She could see him next Saturday night. She thought about him all week long. When she came home there were two calls from him on her machine. She couldn't wait to see him again. They had another special evening. He told her he had worried about her being so far way all week. She laughed and asked "Why?"

He couldn't explain it really, he just liked it better

when she was home. She liked it better, too, she said, but she also liked her job. The relationship continued. They spent more and more of their weekend time together. Then they started getting together during the week as well.

Sex was great, and they truly enjoyed each other's company. They spent a lot of Sundays with his parents, but she didn't mind. She missed her own family and enjoyed feeling part of a family again. Spring came, and one beautiful starlit night, he proposed. She said yes and they went off to tell his parents the good news. Everyone was thrilled. Her parents couldn't wait to meet him, and that's when the first problem started.

He wouldn't fly. He said he just didn't like it. His mother agreed with him, and they went on and on about how dangerous it was to fly. She couldn't change their minds—he wasn't going anywhere by plane, and they didn't have the time to drive out. Of course, this meant when it came time to plan the honeymoon, her vision of Tahiti was out of the question. Instead, he suggested they drive to Maine.

Then where they would live became an issue. He wanted to stay in the same apartment and have her move in. As much as she liked his parents, she didn't want to live in the same building with them. He couldn't understand that at all. Each time they looked at the future, they saw different things. She wanted children; he said he loved children but was afraid to bring them into such a destructive world and, besides, he was afraid of losing her in childbirth. She accused him of being afraid of *everything*. It felt to her like he always expected the worst to happen. Once she was late coming home and he had been ready to call the police.

He was such a wonderful man—so thoughtful and smart, so loving—but she was getting completely frustrated with him. She had never been afraid of anything, but now he made her question herself. Even financially—he wanted them to save every penny because "Who knows what's going to happen? We may need it." She certainly believed in saving, but this way of thinking was foreign to her. Suddenly it seemed this marriage was going to be very serious and very careful. She was a fun-loving, free spirit. She began to question whether it was the right decision. Her uncertainty brought her to counseling.

His Story

His father was in the Korean conflict when he was born. His mother had gone through her pregnancy without him, and it was not an easy time for her. Her husband came home on leave for a week to see his newborn son and then shipped back out. She was on her own with a baby, completely overwhelmed. She had always been timid, and now to be responsible for this helpless creature frightened her completely. Each childhood illness felt like a disaster and it seemed there was always some threat to their well-being. It was two years before her husband came back for good. When he did come home, he chastised her for worrying so much. She felt like he didn't worry enough and ignored him. Life was fragile, and bad things happened all the time.

When her son entered school, she insisted on taking him herself—anything could happen on a bus. She didn't allow him to play sports—too many injuries, she explained to him. Driving a car was a huge issue—not until he was twenty-one, she insisted. She tried the same tactics with her younger daughter, but she would have no part of it. While her son obeyed, her daughter defied her. He was careful, but his sister seemed fearless. He internalized his mother, and his sister reacted against her. He stayed close to home when he finally did move out, moving only downstairs. His sister went away to college and never really came back except for short visits.

The Intervention

She came into therapy totally confused by her fiancé's behavior. She was a woman who lived her dreams. She came from parents who inspired her to take chances, make changes. In fact, part of her attraction to him was that he was so grounded. Her parents were always moving and changing; he and his parents were fixed. Though it often annoyed her, she came to realize there was an appeal about it also. She became committed to working out the relationship and asked her fiancé to attend the sessions.

In their first session together he discussed how

overwhelmed he now felt in the relationship. He loved her but he was weary of her demands. He felt incapable of the changes she expected him to make, and the more she pushed him, the less he wanted to do for her. He said he felt humiliated by her and was no longer convinced they belonged together. She was shocked by these revelations. She had no idea he was so unhappy with her. She had realized only her own unhappiness, not his. Although she had considered leaving him, she had not known she was in jeopardy of losing him. She became frightened that it was too late for them to save the relationship.

To take the pressure off both of them, it was agreed that no decision would be made regarding the relationship until after ten weeks of therapy. The ten weeks ahead were a chance for them to explore themselves and their relationship before making any major decisions they might later regret.

As they began working, it became clear that each held the expectation that their partner would change to suit them. She expected him to become adventurous and daring, and he expected her to settle down. They then looked at how realistic those expectations were. He had always been timid, and as he looked back on his childhood and his relationship with his mother, it became clear why. He had been taught that danger waited around every corner and that his job was to avoid it. Dreams were just that—dreams, not reachable goals. He had never once seriously considered taking time off from work and attempting to write. His world was predictable, and it suited him that way. He had no desire to jump on planes to see the world. There were moments he longed to see certain foreign countries, but his fear of flying totally outweighed his desire. He was content enough right where he was and didn't understand at first why she wasn't. He enjoyed her fearless spirit and her wonderful zest for living, but he didn't share it. He believed he would be a good husband if she just let him be.

She, on the other hand, came from an entirely different background. Her parents taught her that all things were possible, and she was always going after new adventures. She did love his predictability and dependability, but she wanted to inject him with her faith that things are not dangerous and that if you put yourself out there, you will succeed. She admitted she was constantly pushing him to take chances and try new things.

As they talked about their backgrounds and their deepest feelings, it became apparent that neither could change completely. They began to recognize the real person instead of the image they had wanted each other to become. He would probably never be a free spirit and she would never be satisfied with a staid life. The time for compromise and negotiation had come. Once they accepted the other person's right to his or her personal point of view, the battle for control ended. Instead, they began to recognize what they would have to compromise to maintain the relationship.

He felt less attacked, and she felt less constrained. Each made a list of what they thought they could do to make the other person happy and still be true to themselves. He allowed that he would move out of his parents' building. She offered to forgo vacations that required air travel. He came to understand her need to work outside the home. She offered to consider a job that demanded less travel.

After ten sessions they decided to proceed with another ten weeks of joint therapy. They continued working on their expectations and personal differences. For them, negotiation was the key. With her support, he began to delve into his problem with anxiety. He admitted to having panic attacks, episodes where his heart raced and he felt he couldn't breathe. He would have a terrible feeling that he was going to die. After several awful minutes, they would subside. He had never told anyone about them, though he had experienced them since childhood. He began learning deep relaxation exercises and meditation to help control his anxiety. His fear had always been that these attacks meant he was "crazy," and he was relieved to find they were treatable. He also joined a therapy group whose focus was coping with anxiety.

After their second ten sessions of couple counseling, they decided to postpone their marriage plans to alleviate the pressure on their relationship. He continued with his group therapy, and she decided to enter individual counseling to clarify what she was willing to compromise. Her career had always been important to her, and she now had to evaluate what she could give up for the relationship and still be true to herself. They continued to support each other more than they ever had before. Without the pressure of a commitment, they were able to enjoy each other as they truly were. They were willing to let the relationship unfold in whatever way felt most natural and healthy.

The Clues

If she had known about the effect mothers have on their sons, her first clue would have been his stories about his mother. She is so nervous about undercooking the turkey and poisoning her family with salmonella that she destroys the turkey year after year. Laughable perhaps, but insightful as well. When she meets his mother, it soon becomes clear that this is a woman who worries about everything all the time. Put that together with his being her first child and only son and the fact that he still lives in the same building as his parents, and a picture beings to emerge. Another clue is when he tells her that he had wanted to be a writer. Here is a man who has chosen a safer way; instead of pursuing his dream, he chose the family business.

Her next clue is when she goes away after that first weekend. He doesn't just miss her, it also *upsets* him that she is gone. He *worries* about her from the start. This is certainly a clue to who this man is. Then she comes home late and he's ready to send out a search party—another clue to what goes on inside him.

Looking at all this, the rest is no surprise. It makes sense that this man would want to live close to his parents. He has really never left. He works for his dad, and his mother still cooks for him and washes his clothes.

Again, he is a man who takes the safest way. Even flying is too risky. He tells her that right up front, but like most of us, she overlooks the clues and reaches for the love. In the back of her mind she believes he will change when he is with her, as if suddenly this man will want to fly to exotic places, live far away from his parents, and become a writer. Not a chance. *He's* not unhappy with who he is—*she* is.

Another clue she overlooks is his view of his sister. He believes she is wild and crazy because she follows her dreams. Very often in families, one child carries the fear, another the freedom. Similarly, one child might be the player for the family, the other the worker. It's as if the family is whole and each of the members carries one part of the feeling. This phenomenon is called "homeostatis." The theory is that the family becomes balanced, with each family member carrying one part of the emotional body. For instance, in a family where one child is a juvenile delinquent and receives treatment and stops acting out this behavior, another member of the family will begin to act out in an unconscious attempt to keep the family in balance. In many families the siblings are mirror opposites of one another. Instead of *integrating* the different facets of their personalities within themselves, they instead *split off* those facets, and they are shared by the family.

This man carries his mother's fears. He believes in his mother, and he sees life her way. His anxiety cannot be reasoned away by a girlfriend—it's in his bones.

Do's

- Do consider who he *is*—not what you want him to be.
- Do be willing to negotiate.
- Do go slowly and let the relationship take its natural course.

Don'ts

- Don't *expect* him to change; remember, "what you see is what you get."
- Don't attack him for being different from you.

Part VI

Conclusion

19

Making All This Work for You

The foundation of any healthy relationship begins with a deep belief in yourself. Before anyone else can respect you, you must respect yourself. Remember, *you* were given the primary responsibility to take care of *yourself*. It is not selfish to tend to your own needs—it is imperative. Many of us substitute self-care with taking care of someone else. It never works. A man cannot fix your life or give you self-esteem. He can only *enhance* what already exists in you. He cannot save your life or make it safe. True security is born within. Marrying for the wrong reasons is like putting a Band-Aid on a bullet hole. Start by working on yourself. Allow yourself to heal from your own past, then open your eyes and heart to those around you. Give yourself plenty of quiet time. Don't run from your aloneness; embrace it. If you feel desperate for the relationship, step back and examine the *causes* of your desperation instead of hiding them within the relationship. No man can *make* you happy. Your happiness is *your* responsibility and yours alone. When you come from that peaceful, centered place within you, you can treat all people lovingly and then *selectively* decide with whom you want to have an intimate relationship.

Remember, no one is perfect. Most of us have been wounded by life. His problems are not his mother's fault. Like you, she probably tried her best. He may or may not be interested in changing. It is solely *his* choice. But *you* have the choice to accept or not accept what he is. *Listen* to what he wants and respect it. Watch for patterns, and look *realistically* at who he is. Whether he wants to work on himself, his mother relationship, or his relationship with you is up to him. Control what you can, and let the rest go. All you can ever control is *you,* and if you do that, life will become more manageable.

The following list of do's and don'ts can help you stay on track. Read them often. Tape them to your refrigerator. Take a daily personal inventory, and don't ignore early warning signs. It is not impossible to have a healthy, loving relationship with a man, but you have to start by having one with *yourself*.

Do's

- Do be yourself right from the beginning.
- Do ask questions and *listen* for past patterns.
- Do share your inner monologue with him.
- Do keep your sense of humor.
- Do pay attention to the early signs of who he is.
- Do take responsibility for your choices.
- Do pay attention to his family history.
- Do use your mind as well as your heart.
- Do negotiate for what you need.
- Do believe in who *you* are.
- Do act single if you are single.
- Do be gentle with yourself.
- Do examine carefully the "baggage" you are both bringing into the relationship.
- Do use caution if he overwhelms your life.
- Do give your gifts wisely.
- Do believe you are worthy of a special man.
- Do reach out and embrace an offering of love.

Dont's

- Don't let go of your family and friends.
- Don't pretend to accept behavior that is unacceptable.
- Don't shut off your silent alarm.
- Don't bury your anger—explore it.
- Don't think that you are the one who can save him.
- Don't get bitter; get smart.
- Don't think you can change his basic personality.

- Don't fall in love with potential.
- Don't waste years of your life thinking he will change.
- Don't forget the dangers of a vacation romance.
- Don't give up your own life and take on his.
- Don't rush into the relationship.
- Don't slip into denial.
- Don't let him break your heart more than once.
- Don't put him on a pedestal.
- Don't close down your true self to please him.
- Don't be seduced by the familiarity of angst.
- Don't run away from a relationship that can actually work.

ANNETTE ANNECHILD holds a Bachelor of Science degree from the University of the State of New York and a Master of Science degree in counseling psychology from California State University. She is currently a California M.F.C.C. intern. She has authored seven books in the food and fitness field, including the best-selling *Wok Your Way Skinny* (Simon & Schuster), *Steam Cuisine* (Macmillan), and *Yeast-Free Living* (Putnam). She currently lives in Malibu, California.